Patchwork & Quilting

wallhangings

Patchwork, Quilting & Appliqué

Patchwork & Quilting

wallhangings

Patchwork, Quilting & Appliqué

■ **Elaine Hammond** ■

Published by Traplet Publications Limited 1999
Traplet House,
Severn Drive,
Upton-upon-Severn,
Worcestershire. WR8 0JL
United Kingdom.

ISBN 1 900371 17 0

Front Cover
Checkerboard Wallhanging

Back Cover
True Lovers Knot Wallhanging

Book Design by Sue Huxley

Technical drawings reproduced by Paul White

Photography by Julian Morley

Printed and bound by Precision Colour Printing Limited,
Haldane, Halesfield 1, Telford, Shropshire, TF7 4QQ

acknowledgments

With thanks to Avril Hopcraft for sterling work as a quilter and friend extraordinaire and for exercising the grey matter to come up with more hints and tips.

Barbara Chainey for friendship, calm and unruffled advice, hints and tips, and a safe warm refuge when required.

Diane Dorward for reading the instructions to make sure they really do make sense – and for being there.

Laura and Briony Hammond for holding up quilts so I can measure them, fetching and carrying and for not being too demanding when deadlines are looming and Mother is incommunicado.

Robert for keeping the home fires burning and the family fed during my long and difficult recovery from brain surgery. As ever he performed well above the call of duty and made all our lives easier.

Sue Huxley for her cheerful and professional approach while designing the book – she is a pleasure to work with.

To all Patchwork and Quilting readers past and present who have and continue to inspire and encourage.

contents

introduction

Quilts have been around for a very long time, both decorative and plain, and the main reason for their use has always been warmth. Likewise, from the early middle ages, tapestries were used in castles and large houses to block draughts and add decoration. Quilted wallhangings have become popular since the renewed interest in quilting brought many previously unvalued antique quilts on to the market. They are often far too delicate to use on beds or as throws, so are mounted on the walls as a decoration. My first wallhanging, the Card Trick design featured here, was made partly to explore this interesting block and partly to fill a large space on the living room wall! Quilted wallhangings allow you to select the exact colours you wish to complement a room; to create a bold statement far more quickly than could be achieved in cross-stitch or embroidery; and add texture and warmth more easily than with a painting or print.

To make the best use of this book it is worth noting the following:

- *All projects are graded with this symbol*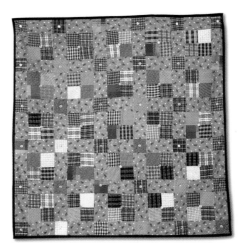

- *1 for easy, 2 for moderate, 3 for difficult, 4 for challenging and 5 for the more experienced. All can be managed if you take your time and read the instructions carefully, but if you are a beginner you should be aware that the higher graded projects will be more difficult and time consuming.*

- *It is assumed throughout this book that the fabric width you are using is 45".*

- *I have used low loft wadding in most of the projects. This is thinner than normal 2 oz wadding, which means the finished project is flatter and lies flat against the wall. Ask for Thermore or Pellon fleece, both of which are available by the yard.*

- *A soft, well worn old cotton sheet makes an excellent backing for quilting.*

- *It is assumed that the usual sewing kit – thimble, scissors for paper and fabric, needles and pins etc. as well as pens and pencils, card etc will be available.*

- *Both metric and imperial measurements are given – use one or the other but don't mix them.*

- *In many cases the designs used will be given on a reduced scale to fit them in this book. Simply photocopy and enlarge them on a copier by the % shown and they will be ready to use. You may need to stick some sheets of paper together to create the required size.*

history

The true history of patchwork as a craft is shrouded in the mists of time. It is known that from the earliest days spare scraps of fabric were sewn together to form another useful piece since this was an excellent way to conserve precious resources.

If this was true hundreds of years ago, it was certainly so when the early settlers went to the United States centuries later. Until they could produce new cloth, the only fabric available was what they had taken with them from the old country. In addition, those settlers who moved northwards were taken unaware by the harshness of the winter and had to create warm bedding from whatever was to hand. It is not difficult to imagine a concerned wife and mother piling clothes on top of her family and the next step would be cutting any good fabric from worn clothing and patching it together. From this 'new' cloth could be made, and warmer bedding created. In Australia this need to conserve was just as important for the settlers there, and the quilts they made are known as Wagga Wagga quilts. In many of these whole garments were sewn onto a backing sheet and added to as and when there was something else available. A case of needs must where the devil drives!

Although patchwork was conceived for the purposes outlined above, there is no doubt that it soon became more than simply a means of conserving fabric.

Too many of even the earliest quilts contain new fabric for them to be solely made from old clothing. In many cases it is obvious that new fabric was purchased to make a quilt, for example when only two fabrics were used together.

Pattern soon emerged in design too and echoes of ancient traditional designs from the home countries were reflected in the geometric patchwork patches or the soft curved lines of appliqué. These designs also came about because everyone has an innate sense of order if not design within them. If you are putting two or three squares together, it is natural to do it in a pleasing way. Designs for patchwork can be easily drafted by folding paper or doodling with a pencil.

Sometimes patchwork block designs are known by several names because they were developed by different people in different areas of the United States who each chose a name for 'their' block. A large number were printed in magazines and newspapers as early as 1840.

It must be remembered however that the old quilts we see are largely the best ones, kept for when visitors came or the doctor visited. Very often this was a bridal quilt which was traditionally made by the friends of an engaged girl or the girl herself. She would have been encouraged to make about twelve quilts in the years leading up to her wedding, since these would provide the bedding for her future family. The quilts were kept in her bottom drawer or hope chest. Whilst these twelve quilts were well used by her new family, the bridal quilt was kept for best, and often hardly used at all which is why so many have survived.

The history of patchwork is fascinating, since it is so closely entwined with the lives of the people who made quilts – often very ordinary people. There are many books written about the history.

Making a modern version of an old quilt in contemporary fabrics can be a challenge for a quilter, and seems to reinforce our link with the quilters of yesterday. If we make a quilt for a family member we feel we are providing

One of the oldest wallhangings featured in this book is 'Ellie Adams Nine Patch'.

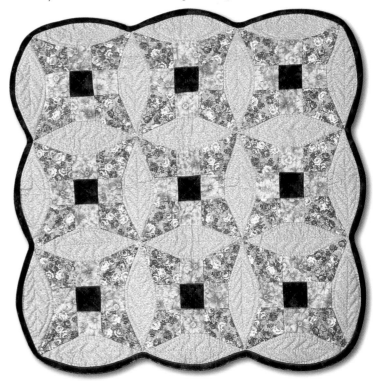

them with warmth and comfort in the same way as our quilting forebears did.

But is this the only reason for making quilts today? After all we can go to the nearest department store and buy a duvet or blankets and keep the family warm and comfortable. What is the magic of patchwork?

Patchwork can be seen as a form of personal expression which goes beyond painting and other art forms. In order to understand this try this experiment:

Take a sunset. It can be a photograph or simply a memory. Try and express its beauty and meaning for you with paints, crayons etc. In one of these mediums you can create a pleasing reproduction of the sunset. Now touch your creation. This is a cold surface.

Using the painting as a guide choose colours to match the sunset from a range of fabrics. You will find this experience taxing, exasperating, exhilarating and magical.

When the piece is finished, stand back and re-live the original sunset. Now step forward and smooth your hand over your work – THAT is the magic of patchwork!

OR: Take as many fabrics, new or used as you can find – ask your mother, relations and friends for anything they have – preferably cotton – to spare. Wash them all – dark colours separately of course. Hang the pieces to dry outside on a line and amaze your neighbours; but not for long, they'll soon get used to the weird activities of a quilter.

Make a 10 cm (4") square template in card or plastic. Cut out squares and sew them randomly together in a way that pleases you. When your quilt top is a size you like from a doll's quilt to a king size bed quilt, tack it together with an old sheet for backing and a blanket in the centre for filling. Tie the quilt by sewing a large knot at the junctions where the seams join. Finally, bind with fabric or bias binding. Also make a little fabric label with your name and the date written on it.

Put it on your bed, enjoy it as it keeps you warm. Drape it on the back of the sofa so it is easily laid over someone who is napping. Place it over the knees of an elderly friend or wrap a toddler in it and rock them to sleep. THAT is the magic of patchwork!

Next time you get a chance, visit a quilt show and watch and listen to the reactions of the visitors. They will gaze in awe at the stunning creations of the quilt artist, gasp in admiration at the perfect stitching and precise corners of the expert needle woman. They will sigh with tenderness and sympathy at the quilts which, although they may not win prizes, stir a creative urge yet unborn; evoke a memory of a childhood with quilts – and warm the hearts of those who can empathise with the hours of blood sweat and tears that have gone into the quilt's creation – THAT is the magic of patchwork! I have been talking about making quilts yourself under the heading of HISTORY. Whilst this may seem odd, it is worth remembering that history is a fluid thing, and yesterday is history.

When you set out to make a patchwork quilt you are indeed part of history, echoing the work of the past, celebrating an interesting pastime in the present, and making a heirloom for which you will be remembered in the future.

card trick

This is a traditional design which is easy to make. The block design reminds one of a hand of cards. Perhaps a bridge tablecloth could be made using this block for inspiration!

REQUIREMENTS

Finished Size: 41" (102.5 cm) x 55" (137.5 cm) square

Block Size: 12" (30 cm)

- 1 yard (1 m) light green fabric for background
- ¾ yard (.75 m) darker green fabric for borders and binding
- Assorted prints in brown and greens
- Piece wadding 42" (105 cm) x 56" (140 cm)
- Backing fabric 42" (105 cm) x 56" (140 cm)
- Matching quilt thread

TO MAKE: card trick

1. Make your templates (see *in a nutshell*)

2. For each block cut: 4 x Template A in light green 4 x Template B in light green 2 x Template A and 2 in Template B in each of four colours

3. Piece together in three rows Fig. 1.

4. Make all twelve blocks, then sew into 3 rows of 4 Fig. 2.

5. Cut 2 strips 3" (7.5 cm) x 43" (107.5 cm) and 2 strips 3" (7.5 cm) x 58" (145 cm) for borders. Cut 2 strips 1½" (3.75 cm) x 44" (110 cm) and 2 strips 1½" (3.75 cm) x 59" (147.5 cm) for binding. Lay this to one side.

6. Pin and stitch to each side of the quilt using a ¼" (.25 cm) seam allowance.

7. Mitre the corners – (see *in a nutshell*).

8. Press the top carefully.

9. Trace the quilting designs from the book and outline in black permanent marker. Place the traced designs on a light source and mark onto completed top using a pencil and the quilting designs as a guide.

10. Sandwich together the pressed backing, wadding and top and tack or pin together – (see *in a nutshell*).

11. Quilt all the marked designs using matching thread.

12. Bind with the pre-cut strips you have laid aside – (see *in a nutshell*).

N.B. Quilt design 1 is also used on the border. Place the heart on the corner and trace the cable up towards the centre sides, bottom and top. Put a heart in the centre of each edge.

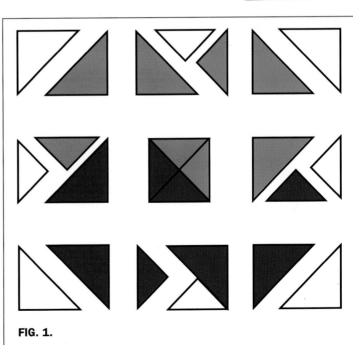

FIG. 1.

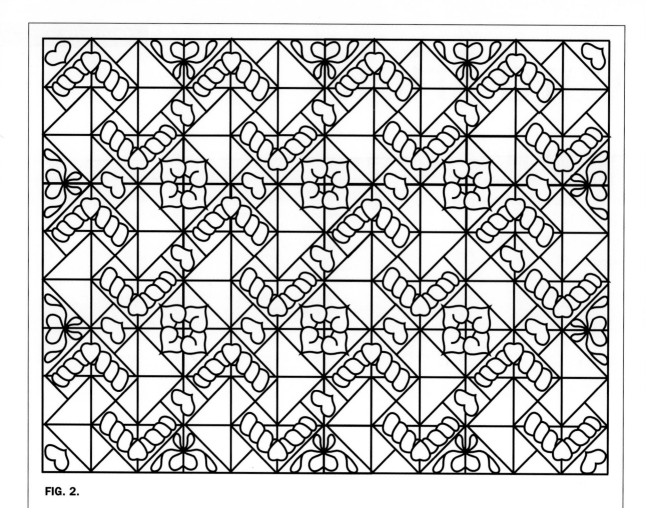

FIG. 2.

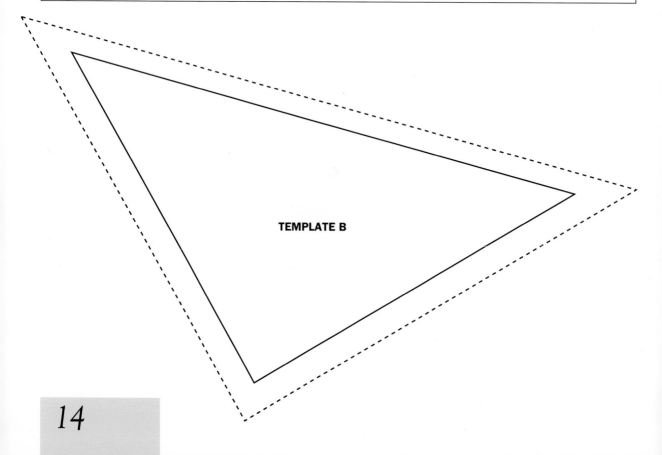

TEMPLATE B

14

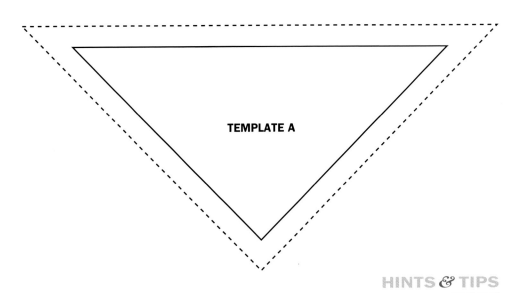

TEMPLATE A

HINTS & TIPS

To avoid bulk in the centre of a block when many seams come together, trim the seam allowances and press firmly to 'set' the centre.

card trick

15

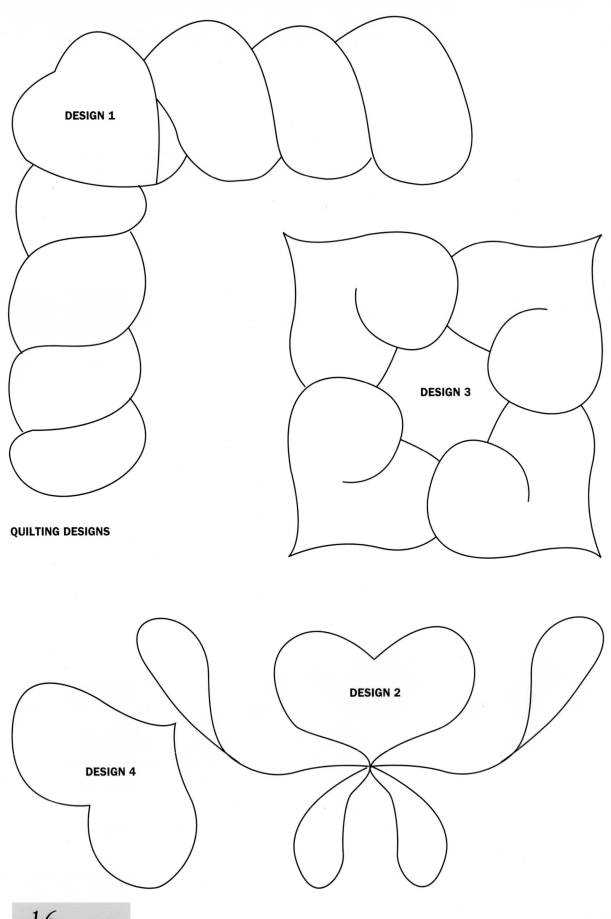

DESIGN 1

DESIGN 3

QUILTING DESIGNS

DESIGN 2

DESIGN 4

checkerboard

Here is a cheerful, very easy to make design which can lend itself to a nice lap quilt too. Try it in different colours, primaries for example or pastels. I found this intriguing bicycle fabric as a background fabric – I'm not sure what else I might have used it for! I have used many examples of checked or plaid fabric – readily available everywhere – but perhaps you can turn it into a real thrift quilt by using old shirts, pyjamas etc.

TO MAKE: checkerboard

CHECKERBOARD LAYOUT

N.B. THIS IS A GUIDE, YOUR SQUARES WILL HAVE MORE VARIED FABRICS IN THEM

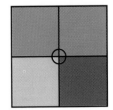

FIG. 1.

1. Make two templates as shown in 'in a nutshell'

2. Using Template A cut 60 pieces in background fabric.

3. Using Template B cut 136 pieces in assorted checked fabrics.

4. Make 25 x squared units by joining 4 squares together (Fig. 1).

5. Now work in rows:

   Row 1 is B A B A B A B A B A B
   A is horizontal

   Row 2 is A Unit A Unit A Unit A Unit
   A Unit A. A is vertical

Press each row after stitching, and try to press the seams in alternate directions on each row. This way they will fit together better when you sew the rows to each other.

6. Now join the rows alternately, there are a total of 11 rows.

7. Press the entire top.

8. Sandwich the top together with the wadding and the backing (see *in a nutshell*).

9. Pin the three layers together (see *in a nutshell*).

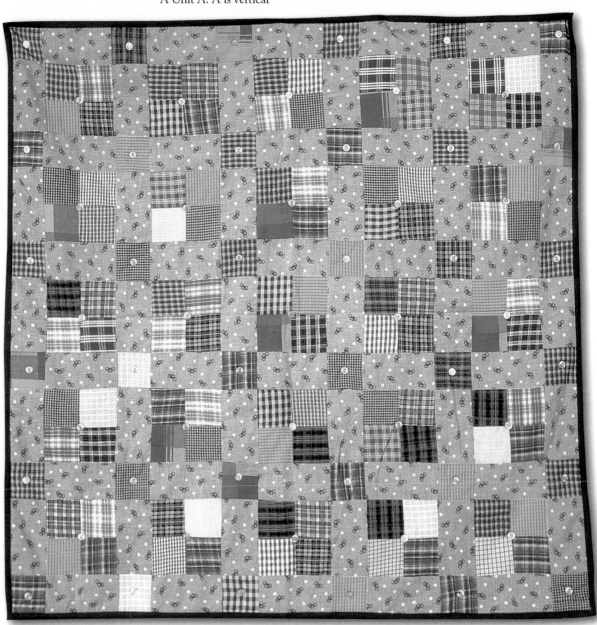

```
┌ ─ ─ ─ ─ ─ ─ ─ ─ ─ ─ ─ ─ ─ ─ ─ ─ ─ ─ ─ ─ ┐
│  ┌──────────────────────────────┐  │
│  │                              │  │
│  │         TEMPLATE B           │  │
│  │   ↑                          │  │
│  │   │                          │  │
│  │   │                          │  │
│  │   ↓  CUT 136 IN ASSORTED CHECK FABRICS │
│  └──────────────────────────────┘  │
└ ─ ─ ─ ─ ─ ─ ─ ─ ─ ─ ─ ─ ─ ─ ─ ─ ─ ─ ─ ─ ┘
```

HINTS & TIPS

Pre-wash all your fabrics to check for colour fastness and shrinkage. This also makes the fabric softer which can make it harder to handle. To redress the balance, try using spray starch immediately before cutting and piecing – bias edges are less likely to stretch, markings may be easier to remove and the piecing will have a pleasing crisp look.

10. Sew a button in the centre of each square in all row 1 lines.

11. Sew a button in the centre of each unit in the row 2 lines.

Please note: in this case the buttons take the place of quilting – couldn't be easier!

checkerboard

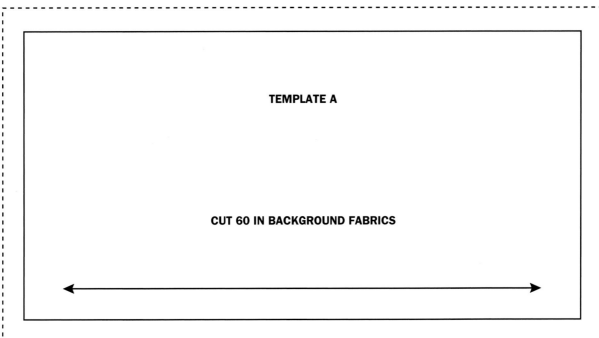

TEMPLATE A

CUT 60 IN BACKGROUND FABRICS

⟵─────────────────────────────⟶

19

drunkard's *path*

This block is well named, the curving design can easily be imagined as the wobbly route taken by one wending their merry way back home after one or two too many!

This particular example was made in the United States in the 1940s. It is made from cotton fabrics and is tied (a way of holding three quilt layers together without quilting) with rayon yarn. You could of course choose to quilt it instead. It appealed to me since this particular pink (known for obvious reasons as 'bubble gum' pink) is so indicative of this time in quilt making, but also because I have yet to meet a small girl who doesn't love this colour. It makes a cheery addition to a bedroom wall.

REQUIREMENTS

Finished Size: 42" (105 cm) square

Block Size: 8" (20 cm)

- 2 yards (2 m) background fabric (pink) (also used for backing and binding)

- Cut 4 x 1½" (3.75 cm) x 43" (107.5 cm) strips for binding and lay to one side

- 1 yard (1 m) print fabric

- Piece of wadding 43" (107.5 cm) square

- Toning wool or cotton thread for tying

TO MAKE: drunkard's *path*

1. Make your templates as shown in 'in a nutshell'. This quilt is made of two different blocks each made of 4 pieced curved units.

For Block 1

1. Cut 52 Template A in pink and 52 Template B in patterned fabric, making sure you leave ¼" (.25 cm) seam allowance and mark the matching notches on each piece you mark.

Tip! You could cut a small notch on the template where the mark occurs.

2. Snip around the curve on piece A, nearly, though not quite to the seam line approximately every ½", or 1 cm. You don't need to clip the curve on piece B.

3. Match the centre marks and push a pin through it Fig. 1.

4. Pin each end then fill in around the curve Fig. 2.

5. Sew carefully along the curved seam taking a backstitch every few stitches in order to help hold the curve. Fig. 3.

6. Sew 4 units for each block and make 13 x Block 1, following the piecing diagram Fig. 4.

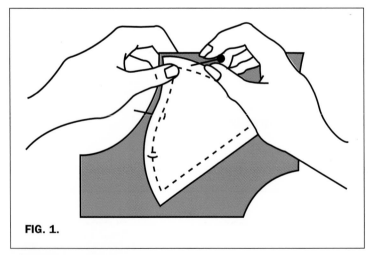

FIG. 1.

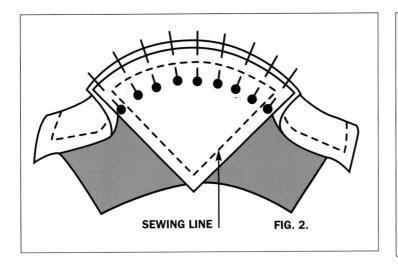

SEWING LINE   **FIG. 2.**

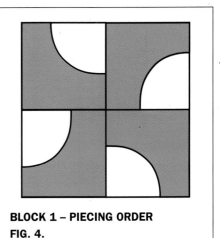

BLOCK 1 – PIECING ORDER
FIG. 4.

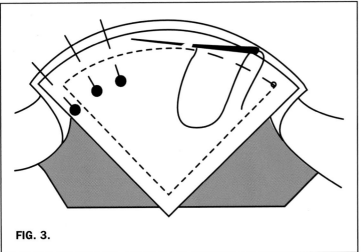

FIG. 3.

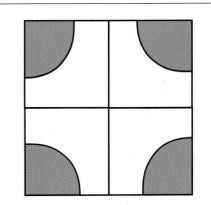

BLOCK 2 – PIECING ORDER
FIG. 5.

For Block 2

1. Cut 48 Template A pieces and 48 Template B.

2. Sew all the units as shown above.

3. Sew 12 x Block 2 following the piecing diagram Fig. 5.

   Sew the blocks alternately as shown in Fig. 6.

   Layer the backing, wadding and pieced top and pin or tack them together.

   Tie the layers together at the corner or each unit using the knot shown below and cotton or wool thread.

1	2	1	2	1
2	1	2	1	2
1	2	1	2	1
2	1	2	1	2
1	2	1	2	1

LAYOUT ORDER

FIG. 6.

*Whatever marking
method you choose, try
it out first on scrap
fabric. Also, test any
marker you plan to use
to check it can be
removed safely and
easily from your fabric.*

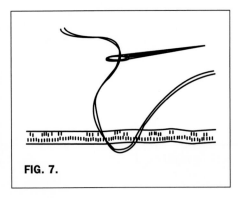

FIG. 7.

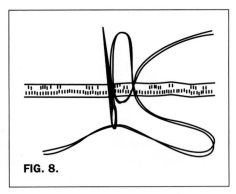

FIG. 8.

Fig. 7 First stitch.

Fig. 8 Second stitch.

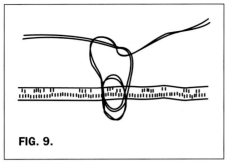

FIG. 9.

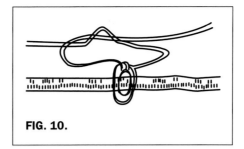

FIG. 10.

Fig. 9 First knot.

Fig. 10 Second knot to make a reef knot.

Bind quilt with matching binding as laid aside
– (see *in a nutshell*).

drunkard's
path

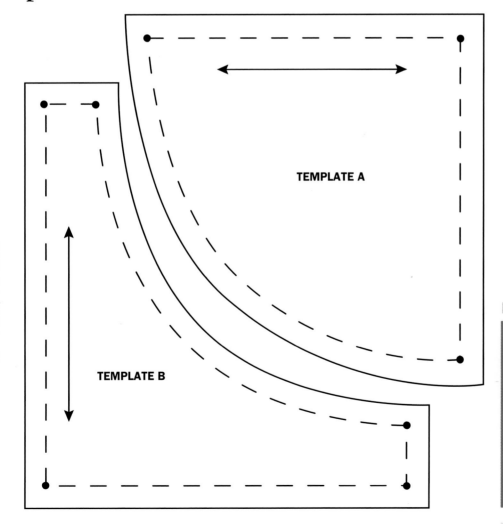

TEMPLATE A

TEMPLATE B

HINTS & TIPS

Water soluble crayons, used lightly are suitable for marking quilting lines. Masking tape is good for "marking" straight lines, but don't be tempted to leave it in position for any length of time – you may end up trying to remove a sticky residue from the surface of your work.

ellie adams
nine patch

This design is a fairly old one, and is usually known as Glorified Nine Patch. When studying this design, I found that by altering the templates to include straight lines rather than curves, the construction was much simpler, but the curves were still very clear. The leaf quilting design, based on motifs found in old quilts, seemed to complement the colours. The name comes from my great-aunt who was well known for being elegant and well turned out. "Very Ellie Adams!" became a family expression used whenever someone appeared in a smart new outfit, hat, shoes or whatever. She sadly died of TB when only 33, so I thought it would be nice to remember her with this elegant little quilt.

Incidentally, this quilt looks very nice over a plain cloth on a round table with the circle of glass on top.

REQUIREMENTS

Finished Size: 21½" (53.75 cm) square

- ¼ yard (.25 m) each of two light fabrics, one medium and one dark
- Piece of wadding 23" (57.5 cm) square
- Piece of backing fabric 23" (57.5 cm) square
- 3½ yards (3 m) bias binding
- Toning quilting thread

TO MAKE: ellie adams *nine patch*

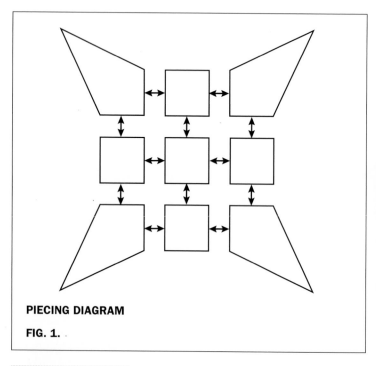

PIECING DIAGRAM

FIG. 1.

1. Make your templates and read detailed instructions – (see *in a nutshell*).

2. Cut the following:
   9 x Template A in Dark
   36 x Template A in Light 1
   36 x Template B in Medium
   24 x Template C in Light 2

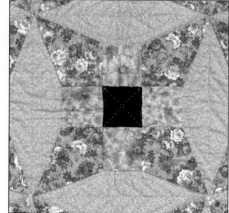

Remember to add your seam allowances to each piece you cut.

3. Following the piecing diagram (Fig. 1) sew nine blocks.

4. Sewing a C piece to the top side and right side of each block, continue to piece in rows of three.

5. Finally add C pieces to the left and bottom of the rows. Press carefully.

6. Trace the leaf quilting design onto all the spaces using a light source (see *in a nutshell*). Using a ruler and pencil, mark a quilting design through the nine patch block following Fig. 2.

7. Sandwich the backing, wadding and pieced top and either pin or tack it together.

8. Quilt along all the marked lines as well as ⅛" (.13 cm) inside the curved edge on all the 'leaves'

9. Bind with bias binding.

10. Add a sleeve and label.

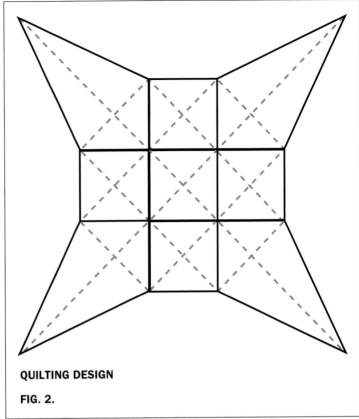

QUILTING DESIGN

FIG. 2.

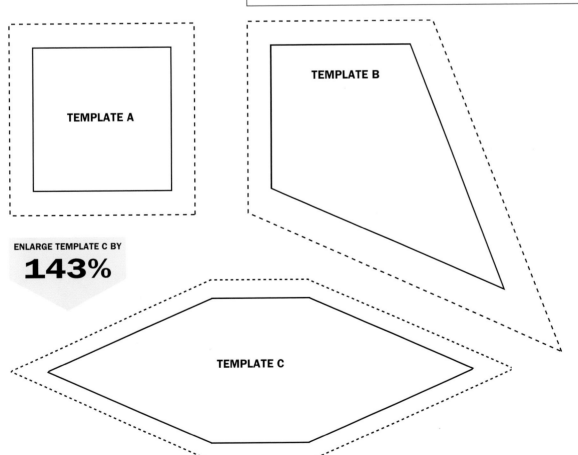

TEMPLATE A

TEMPLATE B

ENLARGE TEMPLATE C BY
143%

TEMPLATE C

25

HINTS & TIPS

A chalk wheel is a useful tool for auditioning possible quilting styles as the fine lines of chalk are easily removed.

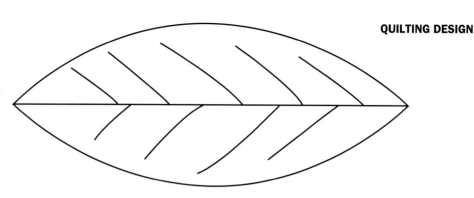

ellie adams
nine patch

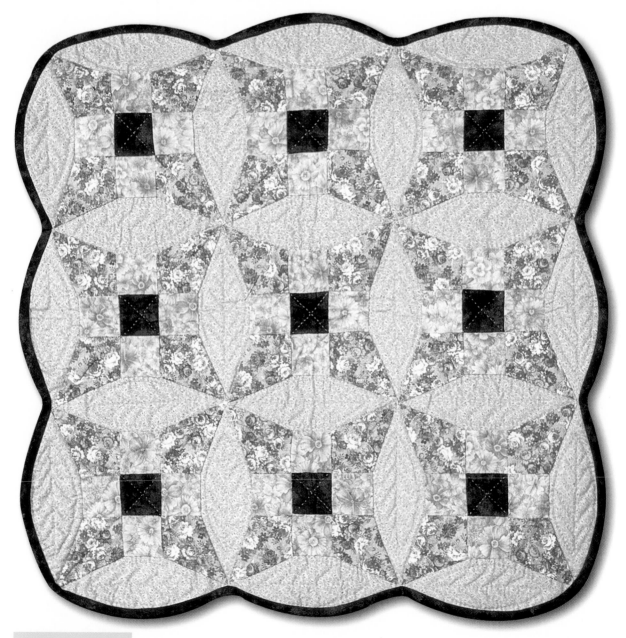

floral charm

I first saw this design several years ago on an antique quilt made in tan silks.
All the tones were similar so although the design was pretty the overall effect was not.

Also the flowers were made from circles of fabric which looked dull, the texture of Suffolk Puffs adds to the appeal. I always imagined the design would lend itself to pastels and I don't think I was wrong.

REQUIREMENTS

Finished Size: 42" (105 cm) square

Block Size: 9" (22.5 cm)

- 1 yard (1 m) each of pale green and cream fabrics

- ⅛ yard (12.5 cm) of nine different floral fabrics

- Scraps of nine different fabrics for the Suffolk Puffs

- ¼ yard (.25m) across the width (not a fat quarter) of dark pink for inner border and binding

- Piece of spare soft fabric – an old sheet will do to make the leaves

- Matching quilting thread

- 1 yard (1 m) backing fabric, preferably light coloured

- Piece of wadding 43" (107.5 cm) square

TO MAKE: floral charm

1. Make your templates – (see *in a nutshell*).

2. Cut 4 x Template A in each of nine floral fabrics. Remember to add your seam allowances!
   Cut 9 x Template B in cream
   Cut 36 x Template C in cream
   Cut 72 x Template D in pale green
   Cut 36 rectangles of pale green 1½" (3.75 cm) x 1" (2.5 cm) for flower stems.

3. Sew the four floral curves to each Template B piece. (See Drunkard's Path project for help in piecing curves)

4. Fold each C piece in half right sides together. Fold a stem in half lengthways, and place the two raw edges approx. ⅛" (13 mm) over the crease. Fig. 1. Pin.

5. Using the crease as a guide stitch the stem into place using running stitch.

6. Fold the folded edge over this seam and slip stitch it down to form a stem Fig. 2.

7. Cut squares of scrap fabric slightly bigger than the leaves (template D). Place a leaf right sides down on this square and sew all around the drawn line by hand or machine leaving no openings. Trim the seam to ⅛" (13 mm). Carefully split the scrap fabric up the centre of the leaf and, using a pair of tweezers, turn through to

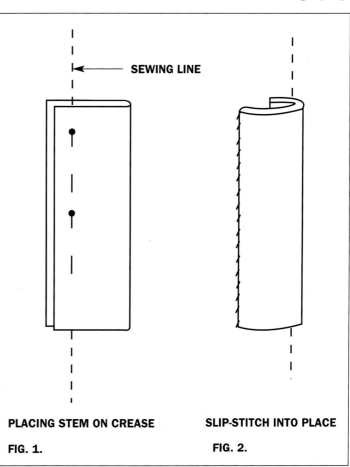

SEWING LINE

PLACING STEM ON CREASE

FIG. 1.

SLIP-STITCH INTO PLACE

FIG. 2.

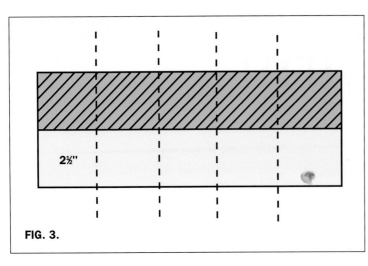

FIG. 3.

2½"

the right side. Press carefully. It is worth doing all the leaves in one session and storing them in a plastic bag!

8. Make four Suffolk Puffs for each block using the directions given below.

9. Slip-stitch a leaf either side of each stem, and sew a Suffolk Puff on top.

10. Place a C piece along each edge of the floral centres and sew into place taking a ¼" (.25 mm) seam allowance. This will catch in the end of the stem.

11. Finish all the blocks then sew them together in 3 rows of 3.

12. From the pink fabric cut 4 strips 1½" (3.75 cm) wide x 30" (75 cm) long. Taking a ¼" (.25 mm) seam allowance, sew a strip along each side of the central square.

13. Cut strips 2½" (6.25 cm) across the widths of the cream and green fabrics. Seam a cream and green strip together taking a ¼" (.25 mm) seam allowance. Press carefully and cut strips 2½" (6.25 cm) wide out of the fabric. Fig. 3.

14. Using the photograph as a guide, join these pieces together to form 4 checkerboard triangles. Sew these to the other edge of the inner border strips.

15. Press the patchwork.

16. Layer the pressed backing, wadding and the patchwork and pin or tack together.

17. Quilt around the floral curves, the square and the flowers and leaves, and in lines diagonally through the cream squares. The three motifs in the centre are available on one stencil no. Q336/3 available from P & Q – see address in Suppliers at the end of the book

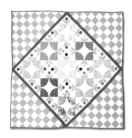

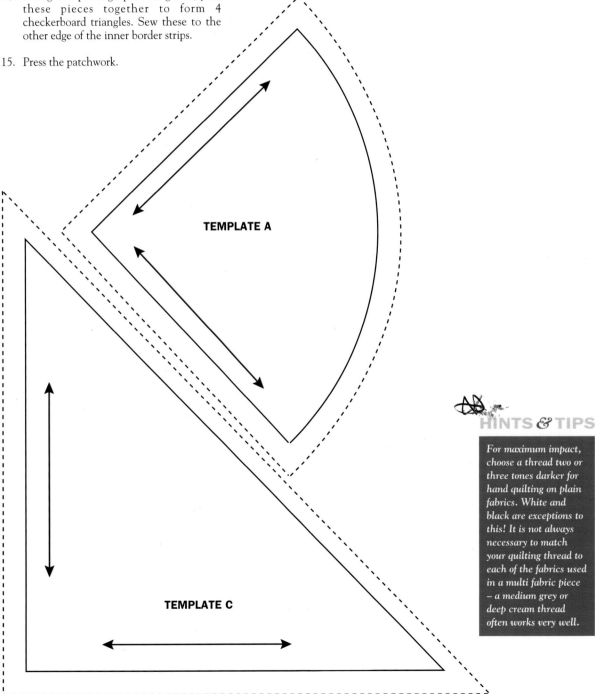

TEMPLATE A

TEMPLATE C

18. Cut 4 strips 1" (2.5 cm) x 43" (107.5 cm). Bind the quilt using these.

19. Name and date your Floral Charm!

To make Suffolk Puffs:

Cut circles 2" (5 cm) across

a. Load your needle with thread and, using it double, tie the ends together in a knot.

b. Turn in approx. ⅛" (.4 cm) to the wrong side and using a running stitch, sew all around the edge of the circle. Pull the thread carefully but firmly and gather up the fabric forming a 'puff'. Take two or three small stitches and fasten off the thread.
Pinch the edges of the puff and encourage it to lie flat. Slip stitch into place where you want it.

floral charm

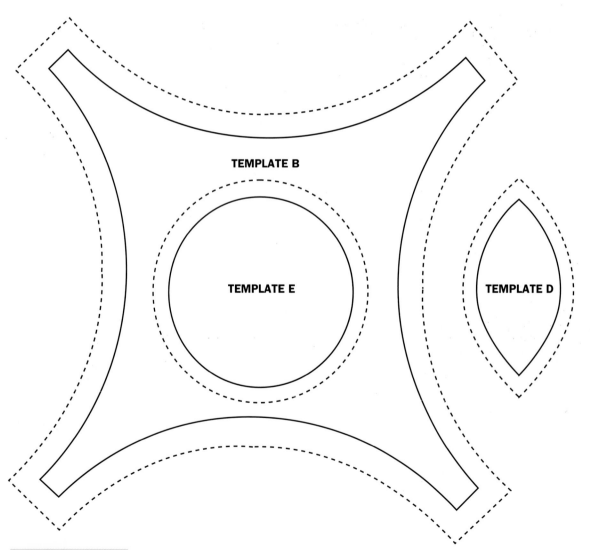

TEMPLATE B

TEMPLATE E

TEMPLATE D

fly, singing bird, fly

This bird design came from a quilt made in Connecticut, USA in about 1850. In the original, the motif was repeated 25 times, which must have been quite boring to work, even if it did result in a full size bed quilt! This is much smaller, but nevertheless reflects the type of motifs that were very popular at that time. I have made this hanging in mostly green and red, again, popular colours of that era.

REQUIREMENTS

Finished Size: 18" x 20"

- .75 m (¾ yard) 44/45" white or cream fabric for background and backing
- .25 m (¼ yard) 44/45" dark green fabric for stems and leaves
- .25 m (¼ yard) 44/45" dark red fabric for flower, bud and corner motifs
- Scraps of dark brown and mid brown fabrics for bird pieces
- 20" x 22" piece of thin wadding/fleece
- Threads to match appliqué colours
- Cream quilting thread
- 2½ yards (2.25 m) 13 mm wide bias binding/1 black bead for bird's eye

TO MAKE: fly, singing *bird, fly*

1. Using tracing or greaseproof paper, trace the entire centre design but only one of the corner motif leaves.

2. Stick the tracing to card, cereal box card is fine. Cut out all the shapes and number them for ease. The greaseproof side is the right side.

3. Place each piece right side down on the wrong side of the fabric and draw around it. Cut around each piece leaving approximately .5 cm (¼") seam allowance around each piece. Cut 4 x 2" (5 cm) circles in red for the corner motifs. Cut 12 corner leaves.

4. Using the marked line as a guide, turn the seam allowances to the wrong side, trimming the allowance where necessary and clipping both the inner and outer curves. Secure the seam allowance by pinning then tacking into place. Tack around all the pieces in this way.

5. Cut your background fabric piece in half vertically and press both pieces. Lay one aside.

6. Stick your pattern to a window or lightbox with masking tape. Place your background fabric on top of this and stick that into place, again with masking tape. Place the tacked pieces into place and pin them into position. This means your background fabric is not marked, and any small adjustments will not matter.

TIP! Ask for sequin or lace pins at your quilt shop. Being much shorter, they are less likely to catch on each other or your working thread.

7. When all the pieces are pinned into place, stitch them down using a matching thread and invisible hemming stitch Fig. 1. Where applicable, place the raw edge of one piece under the finished edge of another i.e. the red flower piece under the green.

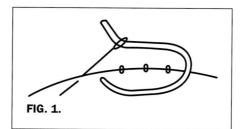

FIG. 1.

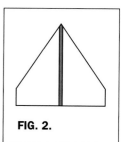

FIG. 2.

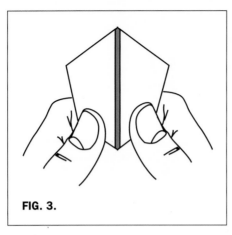

FIG. 3.

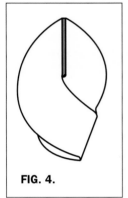

FIG. 4.

8. To make the 'bud', cut a piece of red fabric 3" x 2". Fold it in half lengthwise to form a triangle (Fig. 2). With your fingers poke the bottom corners of the triangle up inside the triangle (Fig. 3) and secure them with a couple of stitches. Fold the two bottom ends over each other (Fig. 4). Pin this under the bud stem and stitch into place.

9. Make Suffolk Puffs for the corner motifs as follows:

a. Thread your needle with red thread and, using it double, tie the ends together in a knot.

b. Turn in approx. ⅛" (. 4 cm) to the wrong side and using a running stitch, sew all around the edge of the circle. Pull the thread carefully but firmly and gather up the fabric forming a 'puff'. Take two or three small stitches and fasten off the thread. Pinch the edges of the puff and encourage it to lie flat.

c. Repeat with the other 3 circles.

10. Appliqué the corner motifs into place, with the Suffolk Puffs covering the ends of the leaves as in the pattern.

11. When all the pieced are sewn into place, press the work carefully and lay it back on top of the pattern sheet. Trace the quilting design lines on to the piece using

QUILTING DESIGN

a sharp pencil, or whatever you prefer. If you wish, you can just mark the start and finish points of the lines and fill them in using a ruler afterwards.

12. Use the cream quilting thread and quilt the design, sewing two lines close around the main centre piece and the corner motifs.

13. Tack ⅛" (.4 cm) from the edge of the completed piece, and trim the edges.

14. Bind using the bias binding and following the instructions in '*in a nutshell*'

P.S. The name for this wall-hanging came from a Victorian song I learned at school!

HINTS & TIPS

When pressing patches, press the stitched line first to 'set' the stitches before pressing the seam to one side.

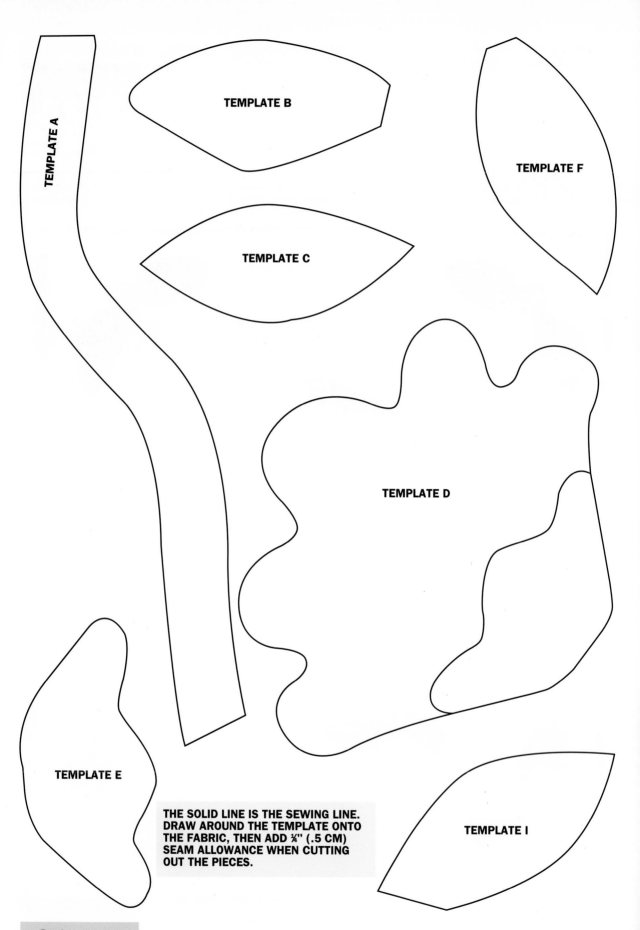

TEMPLATE A

TEMPLATE B

TEMPLATE C

TEMPLATE F

TEMPLATE D

TEMPLATE E

TEMPLATE I

THE SOLID LINE IS THE SEWING LINE.
DRAW AROUND THE TEMPLATE ONTO
THE FABRIC, THEN ADD ¼" (.5 CM)
SEAM ALLOWANCE WHEN CUTTING
OUT THE PIECES.

34

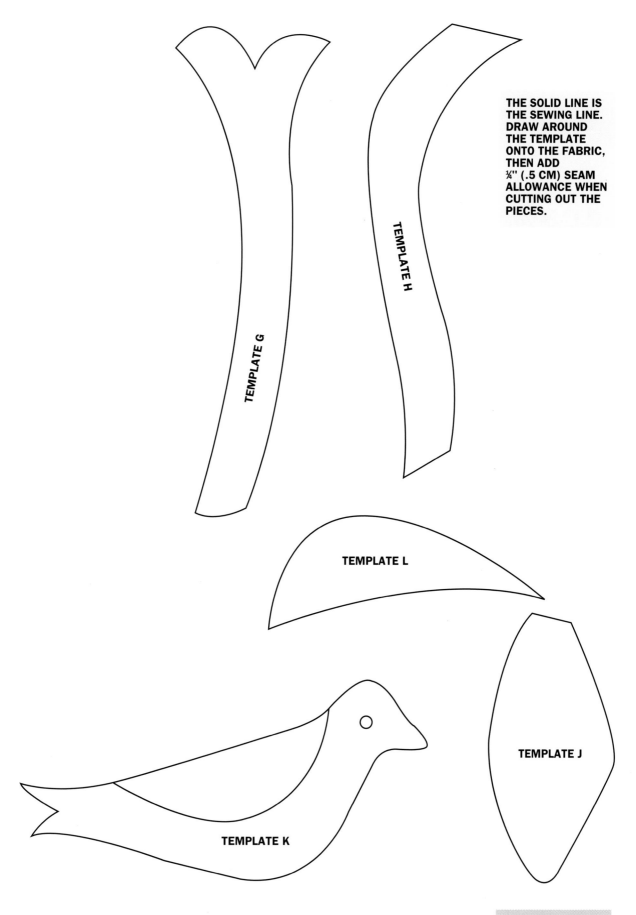

TEMPLATE G

TEMPLATE H

THE SOLID LINE IS
THE SEWING LINE.
DRAW AROUND
THE TEMPLATE
ONTO THE FABRIC,
THEN ADD
¼" (.5 CM) SEAM
ALLOWANCE WHEN
CUTTING OUT THE
PIECES.

TEMPLATE L

TEMPLATE J

TEMPLATE K

ENLARGE DESIGN BY 156%.
ENLARGE COPY BY 156%.
ENLARGE 2ND COPY BY

108%

fly, singing
bird, fly

liberation

After amassing a large selection of varied Liberty Tana Lawn fabrics, I decided to make a single bed quilt in a design which creates a 3D illusion. Jinny Beyer, a well-known quilter calls it Inner Cities, but it is also known as Ecclesiastical and Right Angle Patchwork. There is only one template, a half hexagon, and it can be pieced by hand in the American way or over papers – (see *in a nutshell*). It would probably be quite difficult to piece by machine. I cut out hundreds of pieces for my bed quilt, and they lived in a basket whilst I completed other projects. On a grey day when I was feeling low, I decided that the bed quilt would never materialise and started pinning the pieces to a piece of wadding stuck to our wardrobe.

I had great fun choosing the right combinations of light, medium and dark to get the 3D effect. Having developed the diamond centre and laid aside a quantity of pieces for the border I was still left with hundreds of pieces!

REQUIREMENTS

Finished Size: 66" (165 cm) x 38" (95 cm) square

- Quantity of scraps in light, medium and dark fabrics for the half hexagons
- 1½ yards (1.30 m) cream fabric for the background
- 2 yards (1.80 m) backing fabric
- Piece of wadding 68" (1.70 m) x 40" (1 m) coloured quilting thread
- 6 yards (5.40 m) purchased bias binding

TO MAKE: liberation

1. Make your template (see *in a nutshell*).

2. Cut 75 pieces using Template A – 25 each of light, medium and dark fabrics for centre panel.
   Cut 66 x Template A in assorted fabrics for the border.
   Cut 4 triangles the following size: 31½" (78.75 cm) x 18" (45 cm) x 36½" (91.25 cm in cream.
   Cut 22 x Template A in cream, and 19 x Template B in cream.
   Cut two triangles in cream using Template C.

3. Join light, medium and dark pieces together to form three hexagons and then as Fig. 1, a Y with the dark on the left, medium on the right and light at the top.

4. Spread out the 25 Y shapes and make sure there is a good distribution of colours. Sew them all together to form a diamond.

5. Using the cream hexagons and half hexagons, fill in all the spaces around the diamond. Join a triangle at each end. Press.

6. Add a large triangle to each side of the diamond to form a rectangle.

7. Join the border pieces together short sides together to make a strip. They will not fit exactly along each edge so you will need to 'fudge' a little, either at the centre borders or the corners. Press the top and the backing.

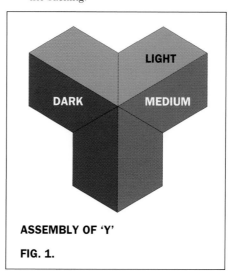

LIGHT

DARK   MEDIUM

ASSEMBLY OF 'Y'

FIG. 1.

8. The quilting design I chose is freehand and loosely based on the design on the curtains. You can do the same or choose a different design. Mark it out lightly with a pencil.

9. Layer the backing, wadding and top and tack or pin them together.

10. Quilt around each of the Y shapes and along the inside edge of the large diamond. Quilt your chosen design in the four triangles.

11. Quilt around the inside edge of the border.

12. Bind the quilt.

13. Add a sleeve and a label.

TEMPLATE B

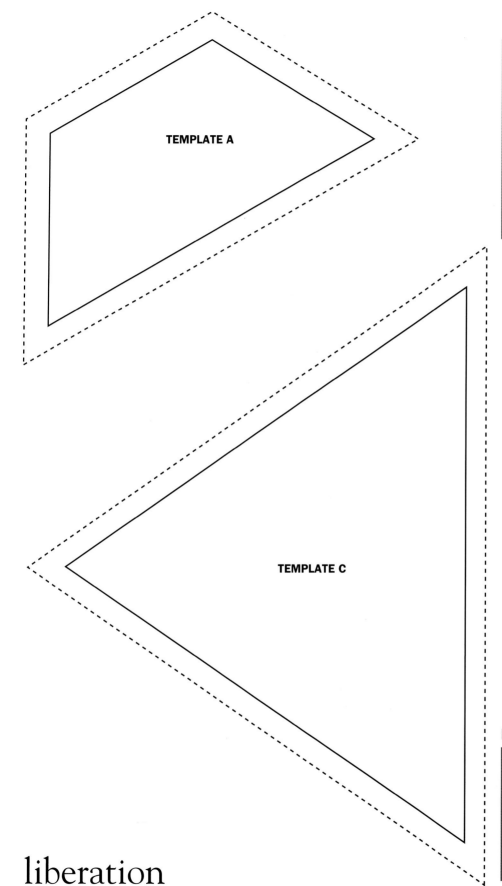

TEMPLATE A

TEMPLATE C

HINTS & TIPS

For maximum impact, choose a thread two or three tones darker for hand quilting on plain fabrics. White and black are exceptions to this! It is not always necessary to match your quilting thread to each of the fabrics used in a multi fabric piece – a medium grey or deep cream thread often works very well.

HINTS & TIPS

Take care if you prefer to use a steam setting on your iron for pressing – too much steam can distort your work, although this can be useful if you need to cajole something into place.

liberation

mountain *peaks*

You can always find room for a little wall hanging like this! Everyone has small amounts of fabric tucked away and you can make this in no time. Believe it or not there are 70 fabrics in the triangles. This idea lends itself to special collections of fabrics – all blues for example or all spots, but you could also include fabrics with small motifs – look closely you will see stars, scissors, a butterfly and a heart.

REQUIREMENTS

Finished Size: 8½" (21.25 cm) x 6½" (16.25 cm) square

Small amounts of 70 fabrics

Piece of coloured backing fabric 9½" (23.75 cm) x 7½" (18.75 cm)

Piece of wadding 9" (2.5 cm) x 7" (17.5 cm)

TO MAKE: mountain *peaks*

1. Make Template A (see *in a nutshell*).

2. Cut out 70 triangles, choosing roughly half dark and half light.

3. Place two triangles right sides together, with the base of the dark piece at the bottom and the base of the light triangle at the top and sew taking a ¼" (.5 cm) seam allowance. Add another triangle right sides together and continue until you have a row of 10 triangles.

4. Make 7 rows and press them.

5. Join the 7 rows together and press.

6. On the wrong side of the patchwork, draw a line with a pencil and ruler through the centre of the triangles of the end rows on the two longer sides, which will be uneven at this stage.

7. Trim along the marked lines to level the edges.

8. Place the patchwork onto the wadding and trim the wadding to the same size.

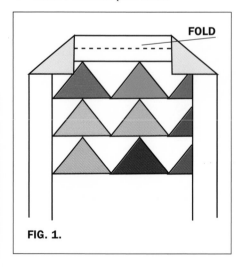

FIG. 1.

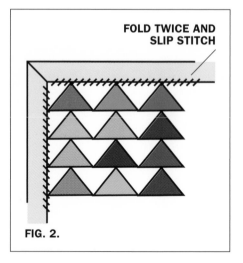

FIG. 2.

9. Place the patchwork and wadding into the centre of the backing fabric. Hold the three layers together with pins.

10. At the corners, fold the fabric over as shown in Fig. 1. Fold the backing fabric over approx. ½" (1 cm) and then again so the fold comes over the edge of the patchwork. Pin into place. Repeat with all four sides. Fig. 2. Slip stitch into place.

11. Rather than making a sleeve, simply sew two curtain rings approx. ½" (1 cm) below the top edge of the back of the quilt.

12. Don't forget that even mini quilts deserve to be signed and dated.

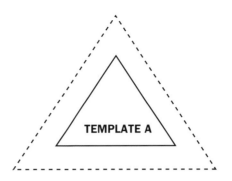

TEMPLATE A

mountain *peaks*

HINTS & TIPS

Change needles frequently for best results in all hand and machine sewing – machine needles become blunt and hand needles dull very easily. Needles are one of the cheapest and most basic of tools so be extravagant.

sigford stars

In 1987 in the seventh issue of Patchwork and Quilting, I recounted the story of Sigford Stars. Here it is:

REQUIREMENTS

**Finished Size: 34" (85 cm) square (for pastel quilt)
42" for larger quilt**

Block Size: 6" (15 cm)

Since both quilts are made using scrap fabrics it is hard to quantify the exact amount needed, but I would suggest you will need at least ½ yard (.5 m) of blue fabric for the background of the smaller quilt and ¾ yard (.75 m) of background for the larger quilt.

Backing fabric: 1 yard (1 m) for pastel quilt and 1 yard (1m) for larger quilt.

Wadding: 36" (90 cm) square for pastel quilt and 42" (105 cm) for larger quilt
Bought bias binding: 4 yards (4 m) for pastel quilt and 4½ yards (4.5 m) for larger quilt.

This is a fairly intricate design incorporating as it does both the curved seam (see Drunkard's Path page) and the star. I place the blocks diagonally and designed the borders accordingly but they could be set vertically. The smaller quilt contains 13 blocks set diagonally and completed with extra circles and 3 border strips. The larger quilt contains 25 blocks.

TO MAKE: sigford stars

THE SOLID LINE IS THE SEWING LINE. DRAW AROUND THE TEMPLATE ONTO THE FABRIC, THEN ADD ¼" (.5 CM) SEAM ALLOWANCE WHEN CUTTING OUT THE PIECES.

Have you ever wondered what original spark ignited your interest in patchwork? Perhaps it was a quilt exhibition, a book or a friend's quilt – but in my case I'd like to think it was a tile! My grandparents lived in this thatched cottage in Sigford, Devon, and I was born in the room behind the second window on the right. We stayed there a great deal in my childhood and there are so many memories linked to their cottage. One memory is of the courtyard at the back of the house which was tiled with star approx. 4" (10 cm) square (see photo) – I can remember my little brown round-toed shoe fitting into one of those squares! It was an attractive design and it can be seen in many places around Devon.

I have heard it called a Devon tile, but really don't know much about it. Perhaps someone has an idea – I would love to know.

When I got really interested in patchwork I kept meaning to trace or rub the design but never quite got around to it. Sadly my grandmother became ill and after her death my mother and aunt went with my grandfather to pack up all the contents. Being heavily pregnant at the time I couldn't go, but asked if someone would trace it for me, but grandad dug up a tile for me to keep. I decided to make a quilt using the design and enlarged it to 6", omitted the channels and placed all the edges together.

It was a very satisfying quilt to work and it has hung on my daughter's bedroom wall for several years. It crystallised for me my memories of that courtyard, and together with the workbox I now use which was made for my gran by grandad during their courtship, it will remind me of a very happy childhood often spent in that thatched cottage.

TEMPLATE E

Since 1987 I have made another version of Sigford Stars (40" (100 cm)) with stronger contemporary fabrics which shows well the different effects fabric choices can produce.

1. For each block cut 8 x Template A, 4 x Template B, 4 x Template C and 4 x Template D.

2. Piece the 8 A's to form a star.

3. Piece the 4 B's to the 4 C's – see Drunkard's Path

4. Inset the 4 D's into the star and then the joined C's and D's.
   The corners and sides are filled with half and quarter stars.

5. Piece the first border in the background fabric (Template E) and the second in a toning print (Template F). Third border is again in the background fabric.

6. In the larger quilt, the second border is omitted.

7. Outline quilt (approx. ⅛" (.13 cm)) away from the seams around the circles or stars.

8. Bind the quilt (see *in a nutshell*).

THE SOLID LINE IS THE SEWING LINE. DRAW AROUND THE TEMPLATE ONTO THE FABRIC, THEN ADD ¼" (.5 CM) SEAM ALLOWANCE WHEN CUTTING OUT THE PIECES.

sigford stars

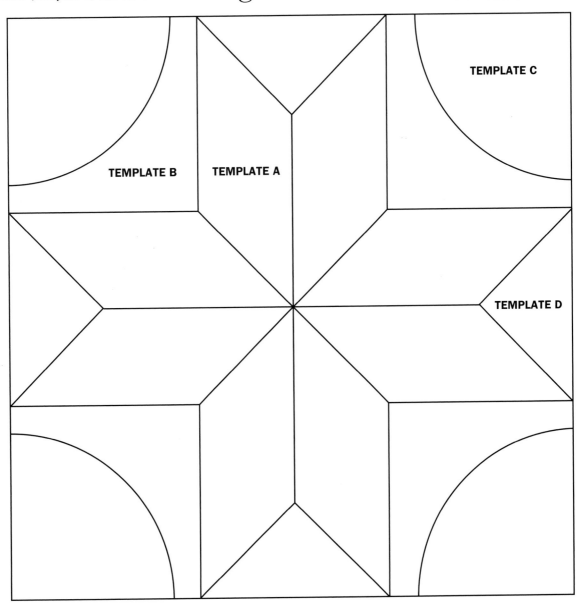

TEMPLATE C

TEMPLATE B

TEMPLATE A

TEMPLATE D

43

TEMPLATE F

44

star *celebration*

There is such a wealth of star designs to choose from, either traditional or those one can dream up oneself, that it seems logical to think of stars and Christmas together.

The super Christmas fabrics with tiny festive motifs will, also come into their own on a quilt like this. There are five star blocks given, though there are nine blocks in the quilt.

Some are repeated, but can be made to look entirely different when alternative fabrics are chosen. Although tricky to piece, the effort will be well rewarded.

Why not quilt or embroider the date in the centre square of the central block as a reminder of when you made it?

REQUIREMENTS

Finished Size: 32" (80cm) square

Block Size: 8" (20 cm) square

- ½ yard dark green fabric for lattice strips

- Selection of approx. ¼ yard (.25 m) pieces in a variety of reds and greens

- ¼ yard each of two yellow fabrics for centre star and border squares

- Piece of wadding 34" (85 cm) square

- Matching quilting thread

- 4 yards (3.75 m) red purchased bias binding

TO MAKE: star *celebration*

Each block is shown below with the correct template numbers on it. Some of the templates may be used in more than one block, so I suggest you make ALL the templates for each block out of template plastic (this will make using the small motifs easier) and put them together in a separate small bag for each block.

N.B. Where R appears after a template number, the template should be reversed for that number of pieces.

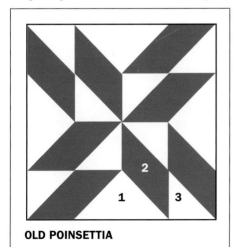

OLD POINSETTIA

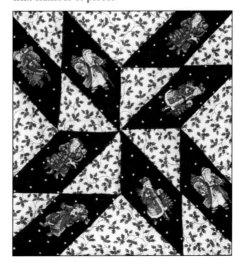

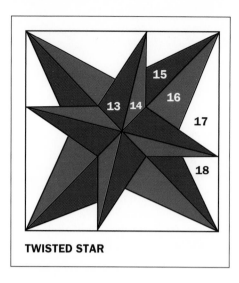

TWISTED STAR

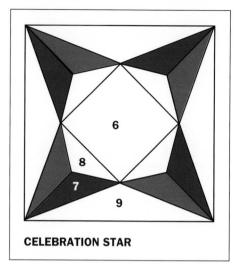

CELEBRATION STAR

Cut as follows:

OLD POINSETTIA BLOCK
8 x Template 2
4 x Template 1
8 x Template 3

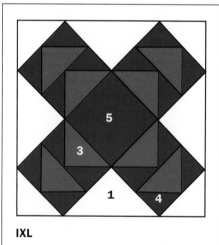

IXL

TWISTED STAR
4 x Template 13
4 x Template 14
4 x Template 15
4 x Template 16
4 x Template 17
4 x Template 18

IXL
1 x Template 5
12 x Template 3
4 x Template 1
16 x Template 4

CELEBRATION STAR
1 x Template 6
4 x Template 8
4 x Template 9
4 x Template 7
4 x Template 7R

GEOMETRIC STAR
1 x Template 5
4 x Template 10
4 x Template 11
4 x Template 12
4 x Template 12R

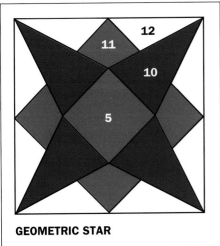

GEOMETRIC STAR

This is a 5 reel project so the piecing order is not given. Plan each block layout carefully before sewing it. When all the blocks are finished, cut the lattice strips as follows:

Cut 24 strips 8" (20 cm) x 2" (5 cm) in dark green

Cut 32 x Template 4 in pale yellow

Cut 32 x Template 4 in darker yellow.

Sew 2 pale and 2 darker yellow triangles together to make a square. Make 16 squares in total.

Join the border strips and squares together as shown in the photograph.

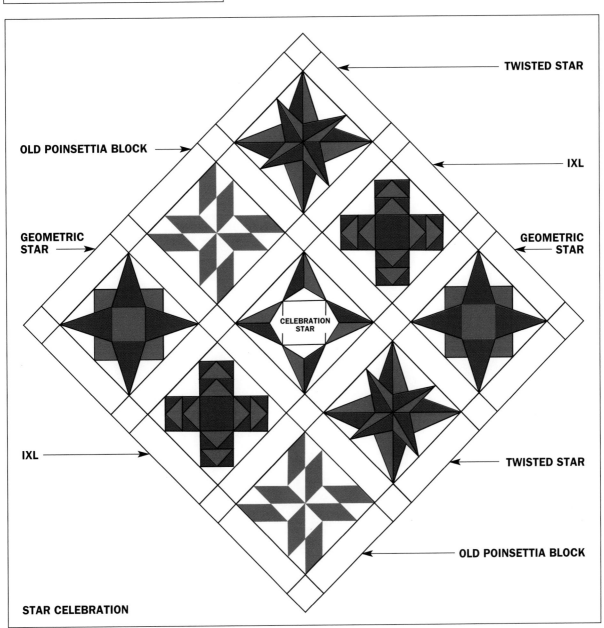

TWISTED STAR

OLD POINSETTIA BLOCK

IXL

GEOMETRIC STAR

GEOMETRIC STAR

CELEBRATION STAR

IXL

TWISTED STAR

OLD POINSETTIA BLOCK

STAR CELEBRATION

When the top is finished, press carefully, then sandwich the wadding, backing and top and pin or tack together.

Quilt around the major pieces in each block and around the outer edge of each square.

Quilt 2 holly leaves (as given in the template) into each dark green lattice strip.

Finally bind with red bias binding.

star *celebration*

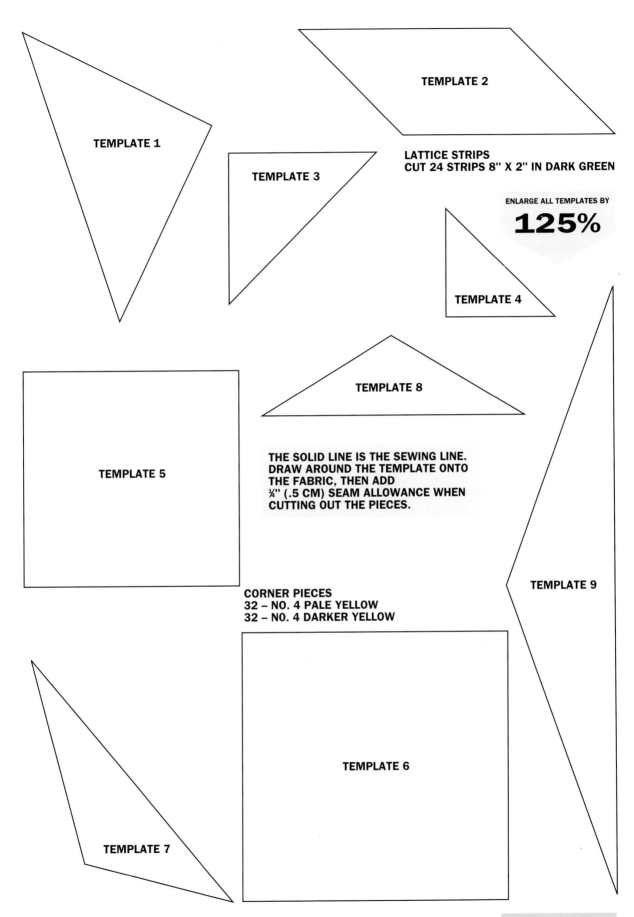

TEMPLATE 1

TEMPLATE 2

TEMPLATE 3

LATTICE STRIPS
CUT 24 STRIPS 8" X 2" IN DARK GREEN

ENLARGE ALL TEMPLATES BY
125%

TEMPLATE 4

TEMPLATE 8

TEMPLATE 5

THE SOLID LINE IS THE SEWING LINE.
DRAW AROUND THE TEMPLATE ONTO
THE FABRIC, THEN ADD
¼" (.5 CM) SEAM ALLOWANCE WHEN
CUTTING OUT THE PIECES.

TEMPLATE 9

CORNER PIECES
32 – NO. 4 PALE YELLOW
32 – NO. 4 DARKER YELLOW

TEMPLATE 6

TEMPLATE 7

49

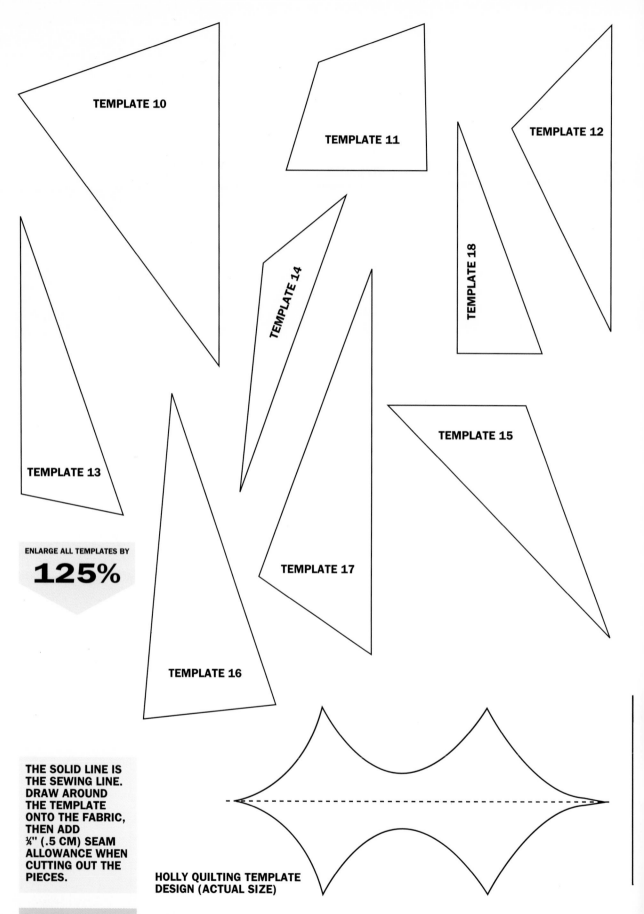

TEMPLATE 10

TEMPLATE 11

TEMPLATE 12

TEMPLATE 14

TEMPLATE 18

TEMPLATE 13

TEMPLATE 15

ENLARGE ALL TEMPLATES BY

125%

TEMPLATE 17

TEMPLATE 16

THE SOLID LINE IS
THE SEWING LINE.
DRAW AROUND
THE TEMPLATE
ONTO THE FABRIC,
THEN ADD
¼" (.5 CM) SEAM
ALLOWANCE WHEN
CUTTING OUT THE
PIECES.

HOLLY QUILTING TEMPLATE
DESIGN (ACTUAL SIZE)

50

starry skies

This deceptively simple block got its unusual name during the American Civil War. It appealed to me as, like the Ellie Adams Nine Patch, the straight lines used together with the Snowball block, creates a curved effect. The quilting design was based on a 'starry' motif found on a quilt made in the 1400s and small flowers found on old quilts from the West Country. The colours were chosen to match our bedroom curtains.

REQUIREMENTS

Finished Size: 36" (90 cm) square	▪ 1 yard (1 m) cream backing fabric
Block Size: 12" (30 cm) square	▪ 38" (95 cm) square wadding
▪ ¾ yard (.75 m) cream background fabric	▪ Toning quilting thread (in this case burgundy)
▪ ¼ yard (.25 m) of each of the following: dark pink spotted print, navy blue print, pale floral print	▪ 5 yards (4.5 m) purchased navy blue binding

TO MAKE: starry skies

To make: This quilt is made of two blocks – 54-40 or Fight and Snowball.

For each 54-40 or Fight block cut the following:

    10 x Template C in cream
    8 x Template C in pale floral print
    2 x Template C in navy print
    8 x Template A in dark pink spot
    4 x Template B in navy print
    Cut out 5 blocks.

    For each Snowball quilt cut:
    4 x Template E in dark pink spot
    1 x Template D in cream
    Cut out 4 blocks.

1. Using the piecing diagram (Fig. 1) as a guide piece together the five 54-40 or Fight blocks. It helps to pin them on to a piece of cloth or polystyrene in the correct order to help you keep track. As you piece each section pin it back into place, and build up from there.

2. Using the piecing diagram (Fig. 2) as a guide, piece together the Snowball blocks.

3. Sew the nine blocks together using the photograph as a guide. Press carefully.

4. A quarter of the Snowball quilting design is given. Photocopy it four times and stick together on a piece of card to make the template

5. The 54-40 or Fight block is quilted in straight lines as shown in Fig. 3.

6. Once all the quilting designs are marked, sandwich together the pieced top wadding and pressed backing. Pin or tack together (see *in a nutshell*) and quilt along the marked lines.

7. Using the purchased bias binding, bind the wall hanging.

8. Add a sleeve and a label with your information.

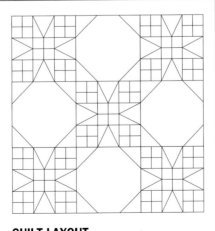

QUILT LAYOUT

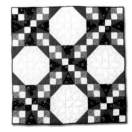

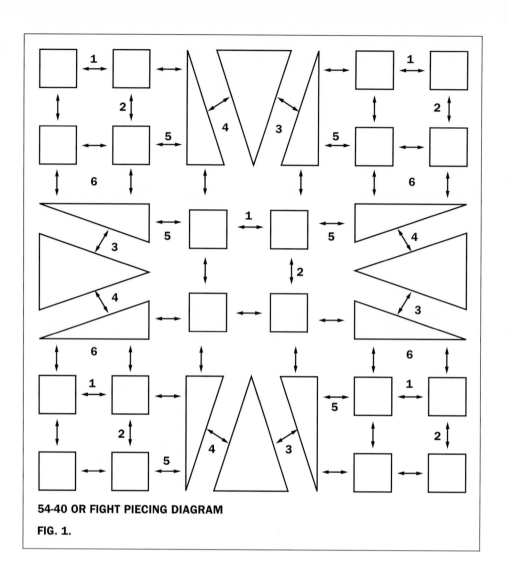

54-40 OR FIGHT PIECING DIAGRAM

FIG. 1.

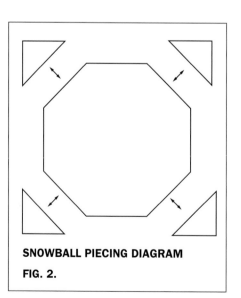

SNOWBALL PIECING DIAGRAM

FIG. 2.

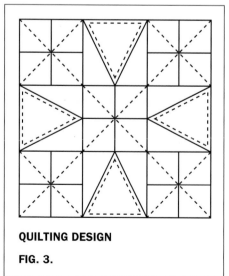

QUILTING DESIGN

FIG. 3.

starry skies

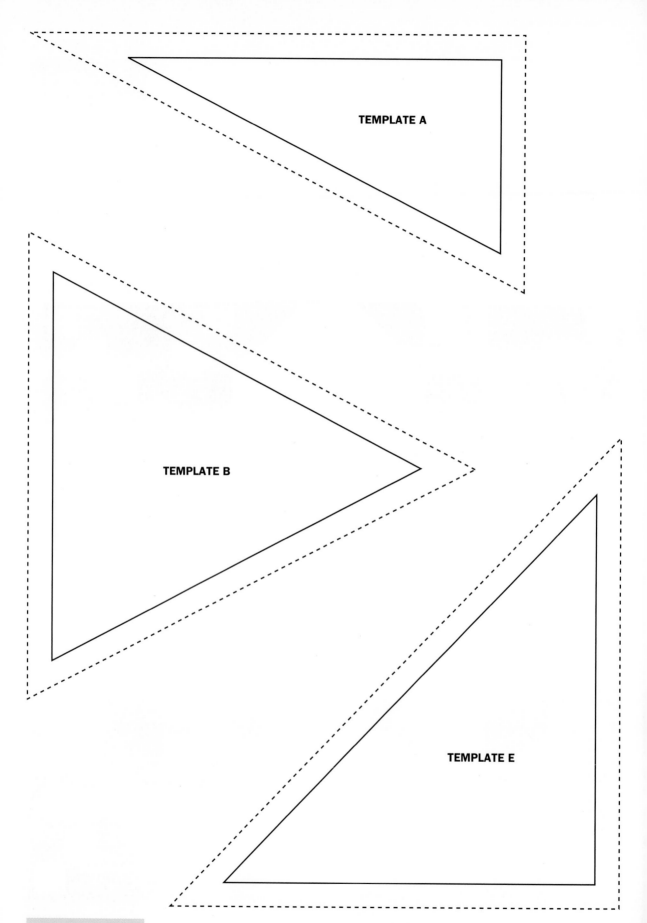

TEMPLATE A

TEMPLATE B

TEMPLATE E

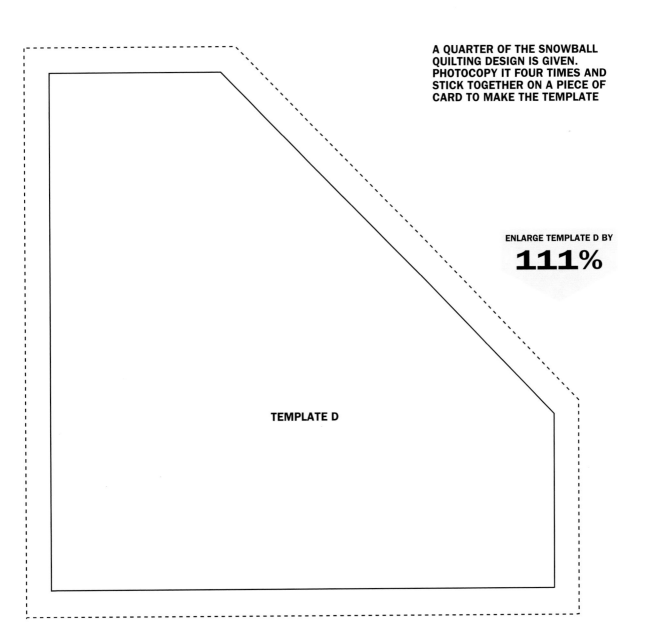

A QUARTER OF THE SNOWBALL QUILTING DESIGN IS GIVEN. PHOTOCOPY IT FOUR TIMES AND STICK TOGETHER ON A PIECE OF CARD TO MAKE THE TEMPLATE

ENLARGE TEMPLATE D BY
111%

TEMPLATE D

TEMPLATE C

HINTS & TIPS

For complex blocks and arrangements of shapes, pin everything to a piece of flannel or a cork board and lift, stitch and replace patches as necessary.

starry skies

QUILTING DESIGN FOR SNOWBALL BLOCK

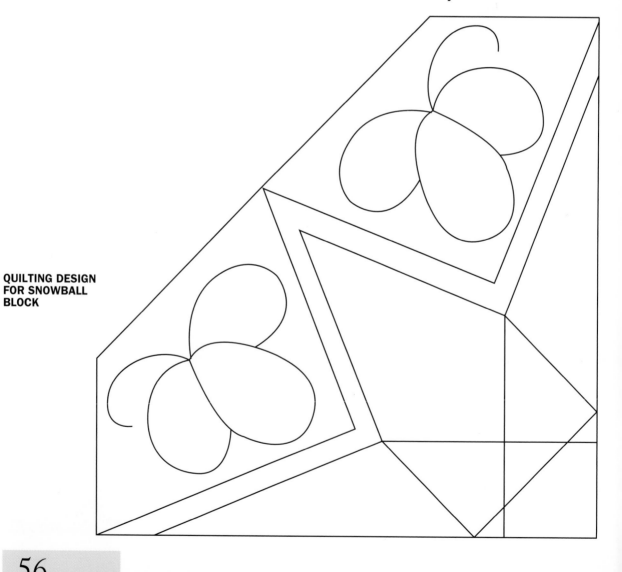

true lovers *knot*

This romantic block dates from 1934 and is credited to a Mrs Danner. The curved seam makes it trickier to piece than a straight seam, but care when piecing the curve will pay off. This design lends itself to two colours rather than a selection though you can experiment. This distinctive design would make a lovely present for a wedding or an anniversary. You could personalise it by embroidering details such as the wedding date, children's births etc. in the curved patches. I have chosen a heart motif for the quilting to continue the romantic theme.

REQUIREMENTS

Finished Size: 124" (60 cm) square

Block Size: 12" (30 cm)

- .5 m (½ yard) of two fabrics
- Piece of low loft wadding 26" square (65 cm)
- Square of backing fabric 26" (65 cm)
- Matching quilting thread

TO MAKE: true lovers *knot*

1. Make your Templates – A B & C and the quilting templates as shown in '*in a nutshell*'.

2. Cut the following using each template, leaving a ¼" seam allowance (see *in a nutshell*) Also, add the marks as shown on Templates B & C:
   16 x Template B in blue
   8 x Template C in blue
   16 x Template A in blue
   16 x Template B in cream
   8 x Template C in cream
   16 x Template A in cream
   4 strips 26" (65 cm) x 1" (2.5 cm) for binding

   To make, follow the piecing diagram Fig. 1.

1. Snip around the C pieces about every centimetre and cutting nearly but not quite to the seam line. This will help the piece curve around the bend of Template B.

2. Match the mark on piece C to that on piece B right sides together and pin through the two marks, then pin each end. Matching the lines pin the rest of the curve. Carefully sew along the pinned line,

taking a backstitch every few stitches to help hold the curve.

3. Now sew the other B piece to the other side.

4. Add the A piece by sewing along one square end of the B piece, then along the other Fig. 2. This completes one quarter of a block.

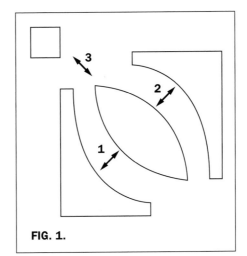

FIG. 1.

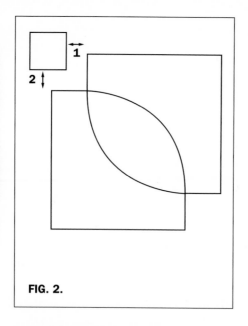

FIG. 2.

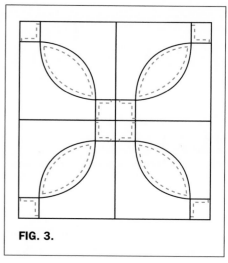

FIG. 3.

5. Make the other three units to make one block.

6. Make 3 more complete blocks, then sew all four together.

7. Press the finished piece, taking extra care in pressing the curved seams.

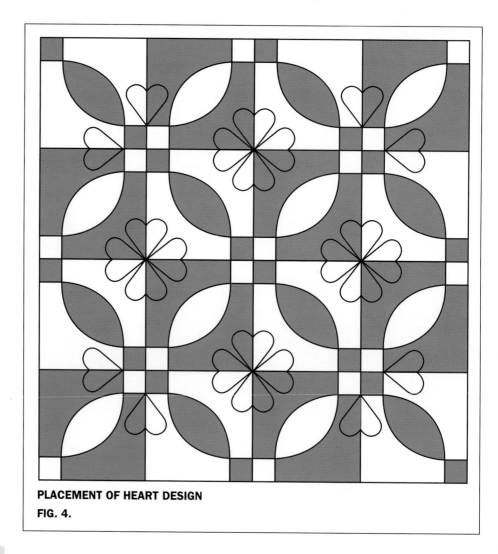

PLACEMENT OF HEART DESIGN

FIG. 4.

To quilt:

1. With matching quilting thread, quilt around the patchwork as shown in Fig. 3.

2. Using the heart template mark the design by placing the solid line along the seam with the point of the heart facing the centre. Fig. 4. Quilt all the hearts.

3. Using pre-cut strips, bind the wall hanging (see *in a nutshell*).

4. Add a sleeve and name and date (see *wallhanging finishes*).

true lovers *knot*

59

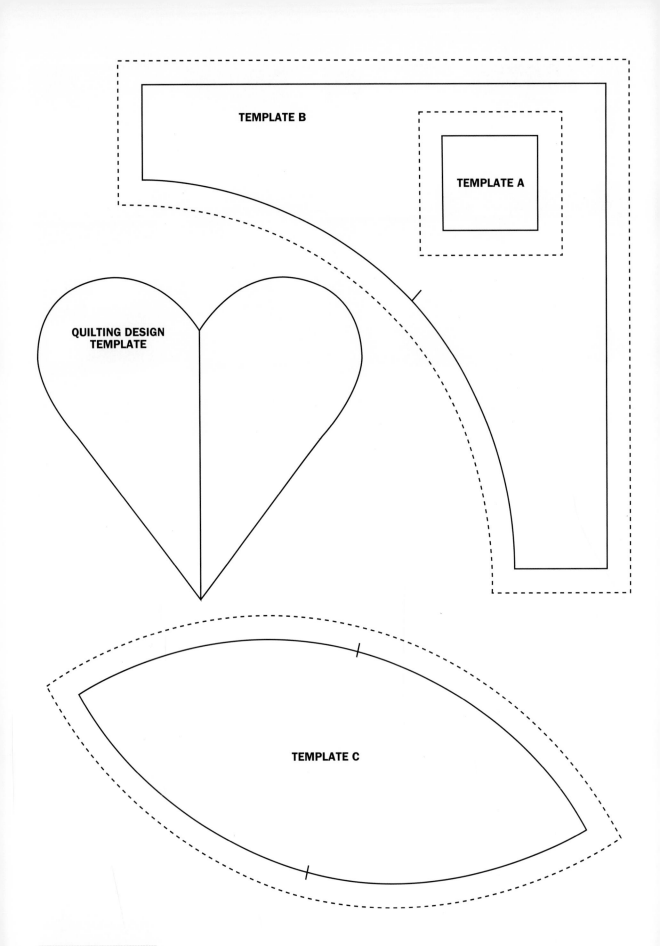

TEMPLATE B

TEMPLATE A

QUILTING DESIGN
TEMPLATE

TEMPLATE C

kate and terry's *wallhanging*

This piece was made by special request for my sister-in-law and her partner. Because they live a long way away, and the colours are particular, I was loaned a lampshade and a piece of carpet to match the colours! This original design is quite tricky to piece, but looks good and has the feel of flowers in a garden.

REQUIREMENTS

Finished Size: 24" square

Block Size: 12"

¼ yard (.25 m) mid-green (1) for background

Scraps of the following:
Pale green (2)
Dark turquoise (3)
Beige (4)
Light turquoise (5)
Tan (6)
Sage (7)

26" (62.5 cm) square of cream fabric for backing

26" (62.5 cm) square of low-loft wadding

Matching quilting thread

1½ yards (1.5 m) matching bias binding

TO MAKE: kate and terry's *wallhanging*

1. Make your templates (see *in a nutshell*)

2. Cut the following:
   4 x Template A in colour 5
   8 x Template B in colour 3
   8 x Template B in colour 7
   20 x Template C in colour 4
   16 x Template C in colour 2

   16 x Template C in colour 6
   8 x Template C in colour 5
   4 x Template C in colour 3

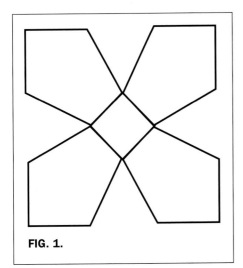

FIG. 1.

FIG. 2.

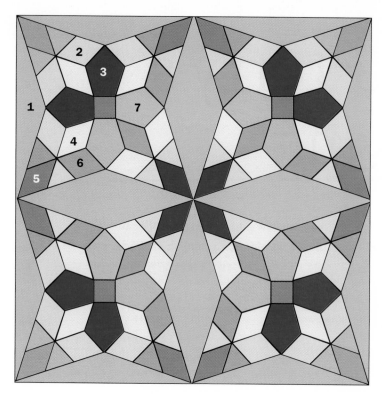

8 x Template D in colour 7
8 x Template D in colour 6
16 x Template D in colour 2
8 x Template E in colour 1
4 x Template E in colour 1 on fold

Tip! It is strongly recommended that you pin out the whole of the design onto a cork board or piece of flannel and work from that. The colour changes within the hanging are quite subtle and need care.

3.   To piece a block:
     Start by sewing two B pieces in each colour either side of A in colour 5. Fig 1.

4.   Complete each point four times in the colours given. Fig. 2.

5.   Join these points to the B pieces already pieced.

6.   Add two E pieces in colour 1 on to two sides of the block.

7.   When 4 blocks are finished, join them with the E pieces cut on the fold.

HINTS & TIPS

When laying down the pieces of an appliqué design, remember to start with the background of the design and come forward, making sure that where possible the raw edges are covered by the pieces on top.

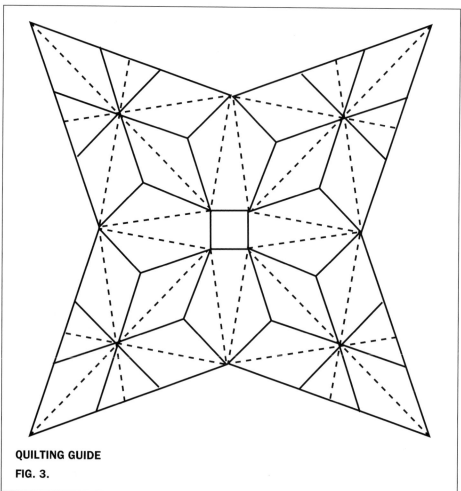

**QUILTING GUIDE
FIG. 3.**

8. Press well.

9. Sandwich finished piecing together with the wadding and backing.

10. Quilt following the quilting guide shown. Fig. 3.

11. Bind with bias binding.

12. Finally, add a sleeve and label to your hanging.

HINTS & TIPS

Add a folded piece of fabric down each side of the tacked fabric to make quilting in a frame easier. Whichever frame you use, clamp it to the border fabric, not the delicate sheer fabric.

kate and terry's
wallhanging

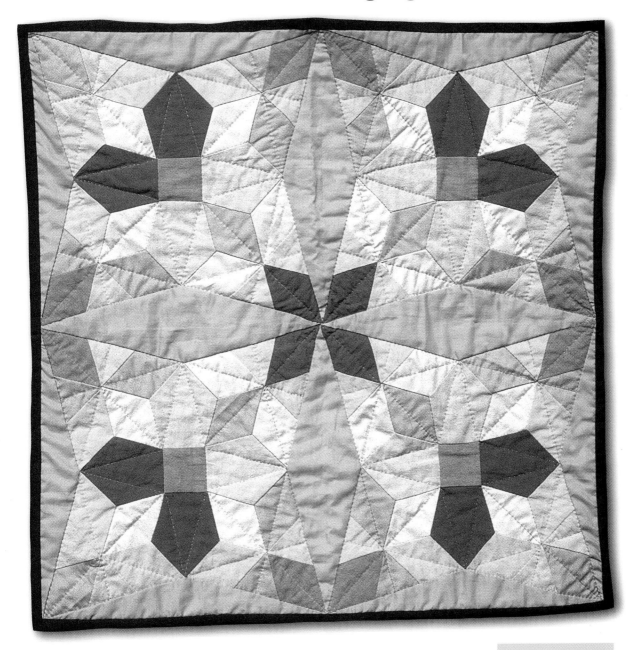

TEMPLATE A

TEMPLATE B

TEMPLATE C

TEMPLATE E

TEMPLATE D

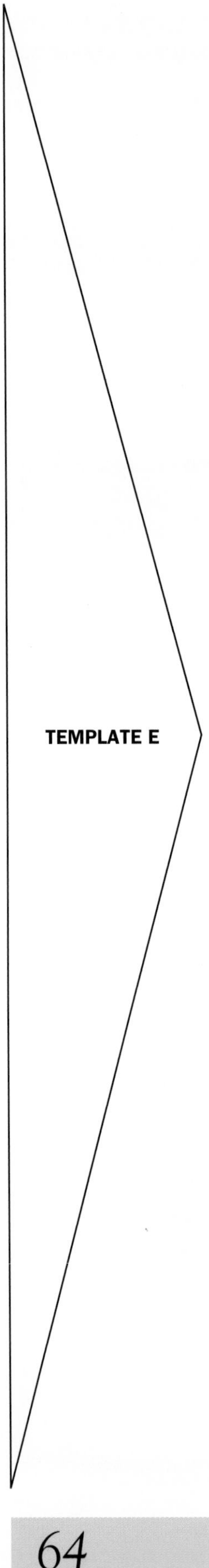

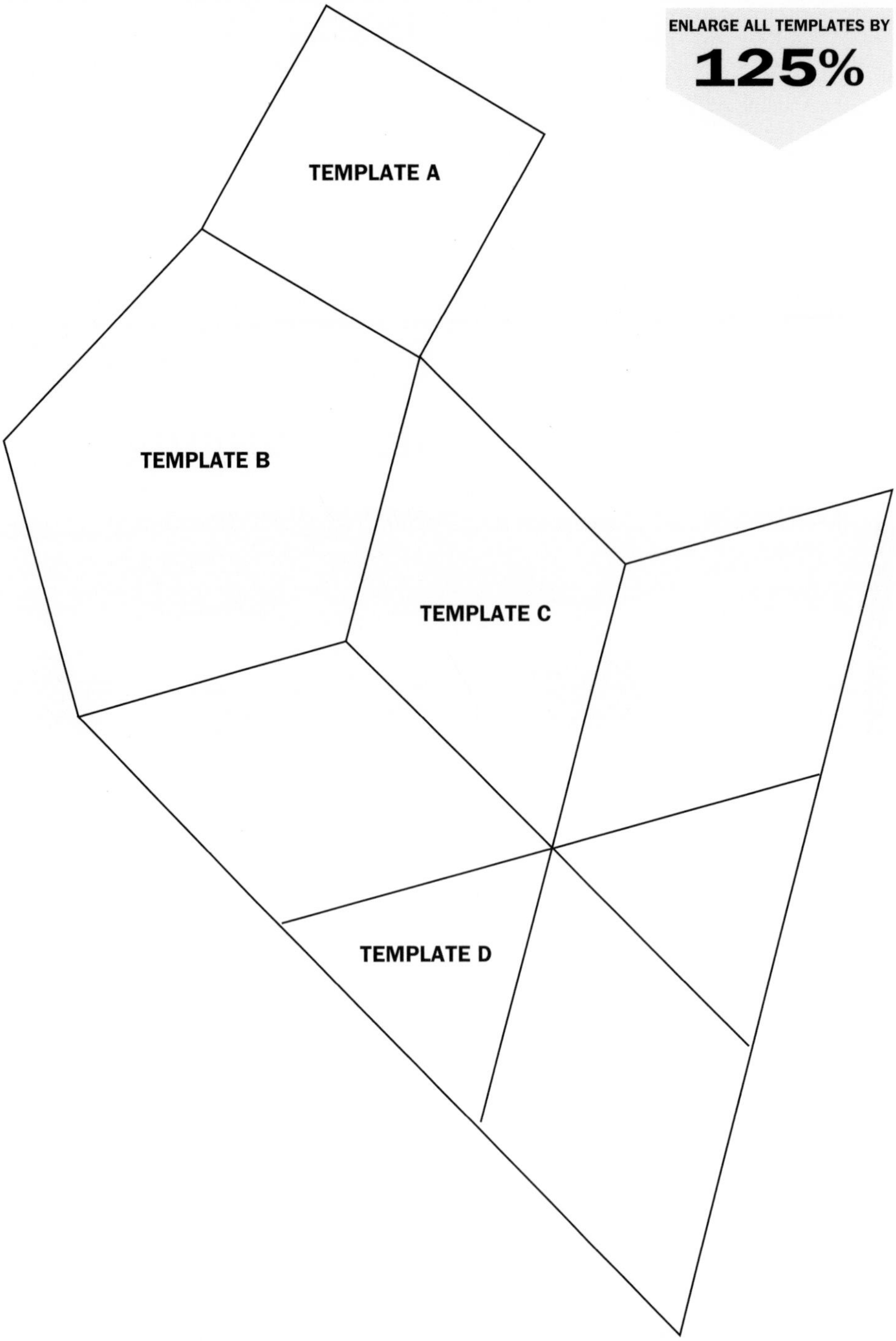

**THE SOLID LINE IS THE SEWING LINE.
DRAW AROUND THE TEMPLATE ONTO
THE FABRIC, THEN ADD
¼" (.5 CM) SEAM ALLOWANCE WHEN
CUTTING OUT THE PIECES.**

wallhanging *finishes*

Make a 'sleeve' to hang your wallhanging as follows:

1. Cut a piece of fabric 6" (15 cm) wide x the width of your wallhanging less 2" (5 cm). If your wallhanging is 36" (90 cm) wide, then the sleeve will be 34" (85 cm) wide.

2. Turn in a double hem (fold in ¼" (.5 cm) then another ¼" (.5 cm)) down each narrow edge.

3. Fold the strip in half lengthways and sew into a tube taking a ¼" (.5 cm) seam allowance. Turn to the right side and press, with the seam in the middle (Fig. 1.)

4. Pin the sleeve into place on the back of the wallhanging about 1" (2.5 cm) from the top, with the seam against the backing fabric. Slip stitch into place along the top and the bottom. (Fig. 2.)

Alternatively you can experiment with different ideas such as loops along the top of the hanging displayed on a decorative pole, or wooden rings sewn along the top and hung on decorative hooks such as those used for curtain tie-backs.

Signing your wallhanging

1. Make a label from a piece of fabric 4" (10 cm) x 3" (7.5 cm).

2. Using an indelible fine felt pen or a laundry marker, write your name, the name of the wallhanging, the date and where you live. If this is a present you can add the names(s) of the recipients.

3. Pin and then hem into place in the bottom right hand side of the back of your quilt.

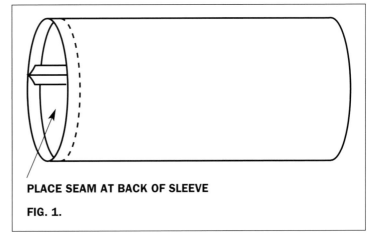

PLACE SEAM AT BACK OF SLEEVE

FIG. 1.

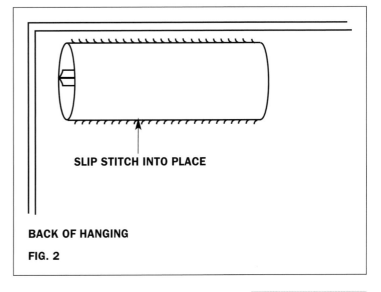

SLIP STITCH INTO PLACE

BACK OF HANGING

FIG. 2

in a nutshell

All of the projects included in this book will have instructions and special hints for that particular item, but the essentials of quiltmaking remain basically the same, so I am including this guide to the fundamentals of patchwork, quilting and appliqué. Please refer to the project in which you are interested for the materials required etc, then use this guide to help you. Read through the information below carefully each time you plan a project, it will help you to avoid making costly and frustrating mistakes.

Understanding Projects

The projects include templates wherever necessary, and by and large they show the ¼" seam allowance required. Should this be different you will be told in the article. The template will have a dotted line (showing the sewing line) and a solid line (the cutting line). These templates should be traced and either stuck to a piece of card, or traced onto template plastic (available from quilting suppliers) then accurately cut out – a craft knife is usually best for this. Be sure to mark them with the size and number of the template together with the project name.

An R after a template means REVERSE. The pieces should be cut firstly with the template the right way up (so the writing is visible) and then REVERSED (writing invisible). Where measurements are given for borders, they will usually include the ¼" seam allowance, but check the project information. Templates for appliqué do not usually have seam allowances included.

Fabrics

Carefully check the yardage amounts given in your chosen project. Cotton fabrics are the best and easiest to work with and the widths available are usually 44/45" wide, but this is not always the case. It is worth getting into the habit of washing your fabrics when you purchase them so that any colour running or shrinkage problems will be reduced. It will also make the fabric softer and nicer to handle.

Marking

Should you be machine piecing and cutting your pieces with a rotary cutter, there will be no need to mark any lines on your fabrics, but you should choose with care the marking used for hand piecing.

A hard pencil kept very sharp works well, and you should run it consistently around the template edges, making sure that you have placed the template along the grain line as shown in your chosen project, and that you are marking the WRONG side of the fabric. Strips of sandpaper stuck to the underside of the template will help to prevent it shifting as you try to draw around it. All pieces to be hand sewn must have ¼" seam allowance added at the cutting stage. There are various ways to mark this line, from a brass wheel to a quilters' quarter, but confidence soon builds sufficiently for you to judge the allowance by eye. Cut out sufficient pieces to make a sample block, and make it up first to be sure that the pieces are accurate; that you haven't given yourself too many bias edges; and that the block comes to the correct size when carefully pressed. When you are satisfied, carry on and cut out the pieces for the entire project.

Piecing

When machine piecing, make sure that you have a ¼" guide to ensure accuracy. If your presser foot is not exactly ¼" try asking your local parts stockist if there is a patchwork foot for your machine, or ask your local quilting supplies shop. Failing that, mark an accurate guide on the throat plate of your machine with masking tape. Adding several layers will actually give you a raised edge to butt the fabric against, which can be a great help. Sew along the entire length of the pieces. When hand piecing, remember that your marked line is your sewing line, and that you must ONLY sew along its length, not into the seam allowance.

Place a pin at either end of the line you are going to sew, and, starting with a backstitch sew along the line with running stitch taking an occasional backstitch to add strength. Take a couple of backstitches at the end of the line.

English piecing: this is the name given to piecing over papers. In this instance the smaller template of the two usually given in such a project i.e. the one without seam allowance is the actual size, and you use this one to cut out your papers. These should be made of stiff paper, and it is very important that they should be accurate. Now use the larger template to cut your fabrics. Place the paper in the centre of the fabric and turning the seam allowance over the edge of the paper, tack it into place (see Fig. 8), starting with a knot in the thread and ending with a backstitch. Once all the pieces have been tacked, oversew them together neatly along each edge.

Appliqué

There are several ways to apply appliqué. For machine appliqué, either use Bondaweb® to iron the pieces into place, followed by satin stitch around the piece, or use a decorative button-hole type stitch to attach and decorate in one go. The notes on machine appliqué projects will go into more detail.

For hand appliqué, mark your design lightly on the right side of your fabric, and then pin or tack the pieces onto the background up in the order that they should be stitched. Sew them into place using either a) a blind hemming stitch or b) buttonhole stitch, taking care not to turn order or appliqué any edges that will lie under the other appliqué pieces.

Pressing

Most projects will need to be pressed several times during their production with the possible exception of silk and velvet pieces. Wherever possible seams should be pressed to one side, and preferably the darker side or away from the area which is to be quilted. Aggressive use of a steam iron can stretch the fabric badly, especially along bias edges, so it is important to either use a dry iron or press rather than iron your work. All the parts of a quilt e.g. top, sashing, borders should be pressed before it is assembled, and again before sandwiching ready for quilting.

Assembling A Quilt Top

Once you have finished all your quilt blocks, lay them out on a flat surface and join them first into rows of the required length,

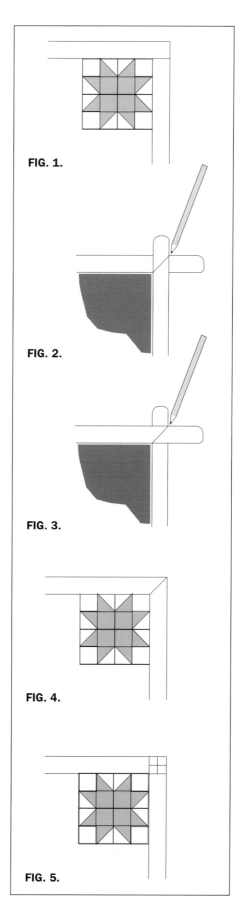

FIG. 1.

FIG. 2.

FIG. 3.

FIG. 4.

FIG. 5.

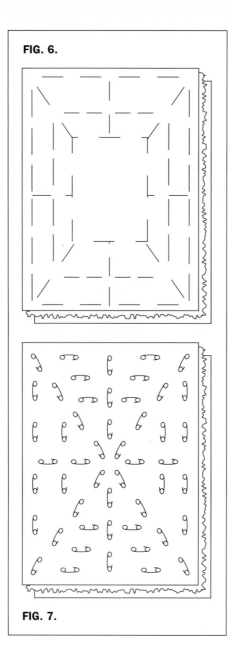

FIG. 6.

FIG. 7.

then join the rows, using a ¼" seam allowance throughout. Now add your borders – first the top and bottom then the two side pieces,

taking care to sew only up to the edge of the quilt top.

Finishing The Corners

You have three choices here – you can square the ends (Fig. 1), mitre the corners (Figs. 2 & 3) or insert a decorative corner (Fig. 4). Should you wish to mitre or insert, you will need additional fabric. To mitre: place one border over the other. Use a pencil and ruler to draw a line between the quilt corner and the overlap corner (Fig. 5). Swap the uppermost border and draw the same line (Fig. 6). Using the marked lines as sewing lines, carefully pin and sew from the innermost to the outer corner. Trim away the seam allowance leaving ¼" then press carefully.

For an inset corner: make a square block, either pieced or plain the size of your border width i.e. if your border is 4" finished width make a small block, pieced or plain, 4½" wide and sew it into place.

Quilting – Marking Your Design

Now your quilt top is complete, you will need to mark your quilting lines. If you plan to simply echo the lines on your blocks, then you will not need to mark, but any extra quilting needs to be carefully thought out. Quilting designs can come from many sources – often a project will have suggested designs, or there are books available both of designs and ideas of how to create your own.

Choose your marking tool with care, some pencils etc may not easily wash or brush out. Experiment with as many as you can find on a separate fabric until you are satisfied. A light source in the shape of a light box or window will make marking the quilt top very much easier, especially on darker fabrics. Any straight lines should be drawn against a long ruler.

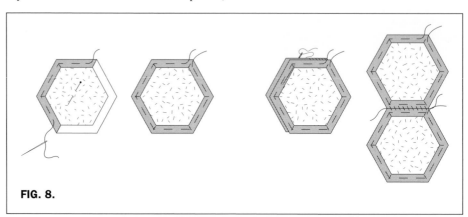

FIG. 8.

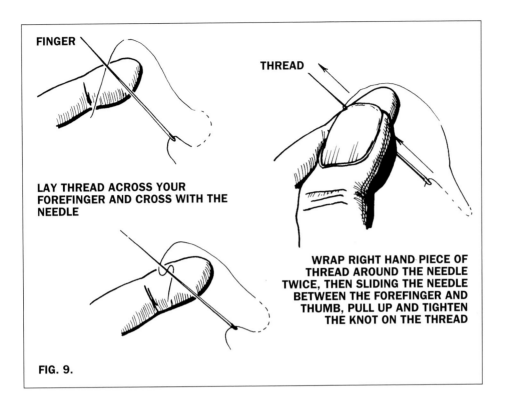

FINGER

LAY THREAD ACROSS YOUR FOREFINGER AND CROSS WITH THE NEEDLE

THREAD

WRAP RIGHT HAND PIECE OF THREAD AROUND THE NEEDLE TWICE, THEN SLIDING THE NEEDLE BETWEEN THE FOREFINGER AND THUMB, PULL UP AND TIGHTEN THE KNOT ON THE THREAD

FIG. 9.

Sandwiching The Layers

Once you are satisfied that your design is clearly marked, and the backing fabric is pressed, make a quilt 'sandwich' as follows: Lay your backing fabric on a flat surface, and make sure it is nice and smooth. Now place your wadding (cut approx 3" larger all round than the quilt top) on top of the backing and smooth that into place. Finally add the quilt top, taking care all the while that it is smooth. There are two ways to hold the three layers together for quilting. Either tack in both directions across the quilt, leaving approx 4" between tacking lines (see Fig. 7 or 2) pin evenly across the surface using fine safety pins. These can be easily removed as your quilting progresses, but the tacking remains until the quilting is finished.

Quilting – The Stitching Technique

The quilting stitch is basically a small neat running stitch. The idea is to hold the three layers of the quilt together in a way that is interesting and decorative in its own right. Quilting is best done with a 'between' needle, which is short and strong. Generally it is believed that the smaller the needle, the smaller the stitch, but you should start with the most comfortable size for you then graduate to a smaller needle. The higher the number i.e. 10 or 12, the smaller the needle. It

is important to become used to using a thimble on the middle finger of the sewing hand because you will not be able to quilt for long without the finger getting very, very sore! Although the thimble will feel strange at first, it is worth persevering – before long you won't want to sew anything without it!

There are several ways to anchor your quilt at the correct tension for quilting; hoops and hand frames being the easiest and most convenient if you want to move around or

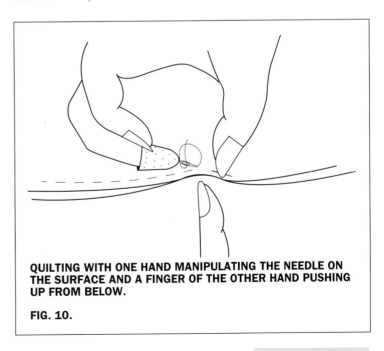

QUILTING WITH ONE HAND MANIPULATING THE NEEDLE ON THE SURFACE AND A FINGER OF THE OTHER HAND PUSHING UP FROM BELOW.

FIG. 10.

pack it away every night. Always remember to remove your quilting from the hoop/frame if you are not going to quilt for a couple of hours. It can leave permanent crease marks otherwise. If you decide to invest in a floor frame you tack the quilt into place and leave it in until all the quilting is done. Try to have a go on a floor frame before committing yourself as they can be a hefty investment.

In general you should begin quilting in the middle of your piece and work towards the outside edges. If however it is thoroughly pinned or tacked, it will not make too much difference.

Quilting thread is readily available in a selection of colours and is the easiest to quilt with because it is fairly smooth and strong and less inclined to knot. Ordinary sewing cotton can be used, but running it through a cake of beeswax will make it stronger and smoother.

Thread your needle with a length of thread, approx. 17"-18", and do a quilters knot in the end (see Fig. 9). Insert the needle into the quilt top, but only under the top, about ½" away from where the first stitch will begin, and bring the needle up and out again exactly where you want to start. Pulling the thread with a jerk will cause the knot to 'pop' through the fabric where it will stay among the wadding. Now take a small backstitch, coming out again just where the second stitch needs to start, and taking small neat stitches, start to quilt.

Place your non sewing hand underneath the work so you can feel the needle when it comes through, and press with this hand to create a firm tension from underneath. You will find this 'under' finger will need some protection too. Aim to place three or four even stitches on your needle at once, so you can develop the rocking motion which makes quilting even and also helps you to relax and enjoy it (see Fig. 10).

When you have finished a line of quilting or the thread is running out, tie a knot in the thread about ¼" from the surface of the quilt, and taking another backstitch lose this knot in the wadding.

When you are satisfied that all the quilting is complete, remove the tacking threads or the remaining pins and you are ready to finish off your quilt.

Machine Quilting

This is becoming much more popular nowadays and there are lots of books and equipment around to help you; they are well worth the investment.

Always practice on small pieces and graduate to larger ones, but do your home work first! Machine quilting can be quick and very effective, but can also be disastrous if it goes wrong.

Binding

Once all your quilting is completed, whether by hand or machine, you are ready to bind your project. First trim away the excess wadding and backing, so the edges are nice and even. There are several ways to finish the edges of a quilt; binding being very popular. You can use purchased bias binding, bias cut yourself from one of the fabrics in your quilt (the bias is essential if your corners are curved). For a quilt with straight sides, a double folded binding is easy and effective, as well as being durable. For this, cut a strip approximately 3" wide and the length of your quilt from one of your fabrics. Fold it in half lengthways with the edges meeting and pin these raw edges along the raw edges of the front of your quilt. Sew it into place taking ¼" seam allowance, then turn the folded edge to the back of your quilt and hem it down the entire length. Repeat with the opposite side, then the top and bottom edges, taking care to neatly over sew the edges at the corners.

To Finish

Now all that remains is to clearly mark your quilt with your name and the date and any other details you wish. This can be done with indelible marker onto a piece of fabric which you can hem into place on the back of the quilt; or you could cross-stitch a nice little label. Don't forget, this quilt could be an heirloom of the future!

suppliers

A Pocketful of Charms
Ingsdon
1 Highfield Close
Malvern Link
Worcs
WR14 1SH
Tel/Fax: 01684 893952

Batiste, charms, shadow trapunto kits, and much more. Send SAE for catalogue

Diane Dorward
27 Hawkwood Close
Malvern
Worcs
WR14 1QU
Tel/Fax 01684 564056
e-mail: diane.dorward@virgin.net

Stencils by mail order, stencilling workshops; rag rugging tools. Send SAE for catalogue

P & Q
Oak Tree Cottage
Evesbatch
Bishops Frome
Worcs
WR6 5BE
Tel/Fax: 01531 640001

Large range of stencils and paints, send 50p & SAE for catalogue

Quilt Basics
Unit 19
Chiltern House
Waterside
Chesham
Bucks
HP5 1PS
Tel: 01494 791401

Large range of tools, quilting stencils, quilting equipment etc. Send 3 x 1st class stamps for mail order catalogue

R & R Enterprises
13 Frederick Road
Malvern
Worcs
WR14 1RS
Tel: 01684 563235

Universal craft frames in lightweight tubular PVC. Floor or hand frames. SAE for details

Strawberry Fayre
Chagford
Devon
TQ13 8EN
Tel: 01647 433250

Superb range of fabrics – Mail order only – send 8 x 1st class stamps for samples

Traplet Publications Ltd
Traplet House
Severn Drive
Upton Upon Severn
Worcestershire
WR8 0JL
Tel: +44 (0) 1684 594505
Fax: + 44 (0) 1684 594586
Email: general@traplet.co.uk
Website: www.traplet.co.uk

Patchwork & Quilting
The First & Best Loved Magazine For The True Enthusiast!
This bi-monthly magazine captures the fascination that quilting has held for millions of people over 100s of years. Projects, show reports, new products, competitions and a multitude of hints and tips

£2.95 Bi-Monthly
Available the third Friday of every other month

Sewing World
Dedicated to machine stitchers the world over, Sewing World magazine has experienced an explosion in popularity since its launch in Spring '95. From making outfits, to furnishings, the care of fabrics and how to get the most from your sewing machine, Sewing World has it all. Bursting with inspirational ideas and packed with useful tips, it's the essential companion for every machine sewing enthusiast

£2.75 Monthly
Available the third Friday of every month

Both of these magazines are available from all good newsagents and craft shops or direct from Traplet Publications

other titles

Patchwork & Quilting CUSHIONS by Elaine Hammond
Here is an amazing selection of cushions using patchwork quilting and appliqué.
Inspiration abounds – and there are full instructions, templates, colour ideas and a host of hints and tips.
Follow the patterns precisely or enjoy exploring your own ideas using the many techniques to which you will be introduced.
A perfect present for a friend – or yourself!

Mastering Your Sewing Machine by Myra Coles
The guide to mastering your sewing machine! Whatever your sewing expertise, it is essential that you know how it will respond in all sewing circumstances. Until your machine is an extension of your own fingers and working 'as one' with you, it is impossible to get the very best from it.

Available from:
U.K. and international enquiries:
Traplet Publications Ltd.,
Traplet House,
Severn Drive,
Upton-upon-Severn,
Worcestershire,
WR8 0JL
Tel: +44 (0) 1684 594505
Fax: +44 (0) 1684 594586
Email: general@traplet.co.uk
Website: www.traplet.co.uk

U.S.A. enquiries:
Traplet Distribution USA Limited.,
3103 Tatman Court,
Suite 105,
Urbana,
IL 61802
U.S.A.
Tel: (217) 328 4444
Fax: (217) 328 2450
Email: info@traplet.com
Website: www.traplet.com

Look out for these exciting forthcoming titles:

Patchwork & Quilting
CHRISTMAS

Patchwork & Quilting
TRADITIONAL QUILTS

Patchwork & Quilting
PROJECTS FOR CHILDREN